Drive for Show,
Putt for Dough

Drive for Show, Putt for Dough

Memoirs of a Golf Hustler

LEON CRUMP *and*
JOHN STRAVINSKY

HarperCollins*Publishers*

*For Peg,
and my children—
Bobby, Susan, and Jamie*

HarperCollins books may be purchased for educational, business, or sales promotional use. For information please write: Special Markets Department, HarperCollins Publishers, Inc., 10 East 53rd Street, New York, NY 10022.

FIRST EDITION

Designed by Irving Perkins Associates, Inc.

Library of Congress Cataloging-in-Publication Data

Crump, Leon, 1935–
    Drive for show, putt for dough : memoirs of a golf hustler / Leon Crump and John Stravinsky. — 1st ed.
        p.   cm.
    ISBN 0-06-270171-1
    1. Crump, Leon, 1935–   . 2. Golfers—United States—Biography. 3. Sports betting.   I. Stravinsky, John. II. Title.
    GV964.C78A3   1997
    796.352'092—dc21
    [B]   97-2423

97 98 99 00 01 ❖/RRD 10 9 8 7 6 5 4 3 2 1

Contents

Contents

Preface

I first met Leon Crump four years ago when I was working on a story for a national magazine about Michael Jordan's high-stakes golf games in the Carolinas. My investigative trail didn't exactly lead to Leon, although it turned out he knew most of Jordan's beneficiaries. What drew me to Crump was his reputation in the area as the "greatest money player who ever lived." I was intrigued. Who was this guy whose name seemed to come up in any mention of top-dollar golf action, and what was it about a golf hustler from Charlotte that evoked such downright reverence among those who knew him?

Even if he couldn't give me much on Jordan, I was immediately taken by Leon's style and his unique calling. "I guess it's like a job," he told me, while he waited by a clubhouse pay phone for word of whether a $500 match, "up in the mountains," was on or off for that afternoon. When I prodded, Leon admitted that he'd given up his actual day job some thirty-five years earlier and had made a living at "golf games" ever since. To a 10-handicapper prone to blowing putts for bets in the single figures, this was heady stuff.

Not that there's necessarily a stereotype, but with his conservative golf clothes, humble manner, and Coke-bottle thick glasses, Leon seemed decidedly unhustlerlike. (I would later realize that winning big bucks on the links has little to do with flash, dash, or running of the mouth.) On the subject of Jordan's golf bets, Leon spoke candidly that day about how people should be allowed to do what they wanted to with their money. He also avowed that while he hadn't been involved in any of Michael's golf action, he certainly wouldn't have minded taking part. I could almost detect the proverbial twinkle in his eye.

We stayed in touch and a couple of years later, we set out to tell his story—"professional" golf of a different bent. Over our days of taped interviews, Leon spilled tales from the underside of a fascinating subculture. Since he was far too modest to expound on his own personal exploits, it remained for characters from his past to tell me how extraordinary his talents were.

An ex–road partner would call Leon "the best there ever was at playing from the dead muscle," a term for spectacular, full-bore shot-making ability. A newsman from St. Petersburg, Florida, would recall Leon's eleven consecutive birdies at a satellite tournament, also watching him shoot 61 to win $6,000 from a Bible salesman who was "scrambling" four balls (*selecting the best of four tries on each shot*). A Mobile lawyer (and sometime golf victim) would opine that "at one time, Leon Crump could beat anyone in the world at match play"—which might explain another crony's recollection of how Crump used to fantasize playing Jack Nicklaus, one match, head-up, for $1,000,000.

There were tales of impossible shots, successful or not, of near-par rounds using only a putter, of par-5 holes nearly-reached with a single drive. Leon's longtime partner Dickie Starnes shook his head at the memory of one unforgettable wedge shot worth a suitcase of money: "We must have had twenty bets, and now he's in the middle of a friggin' forest, 100 foot high treeline, about 120 yards from the green. I said, 'what are you gonna do?' He said, 'Knock it over the trees up onto the green.' I said 'Dang, ain't no way.' He must of hit that s.o.b. as high as he did long and landed it right against the flagstick. Those guys never did recover."

Starnes also echoed a line I had heard from others, that many of the people who played Leon over the years didn't really care if they won or lost: "They just wanted to say they played with him. The money was besides the point."

However, that didn't always hold true. In conversations with different sources, I heard stories of how Leon had clipped a couple of very famous professional golfers—past U.S. Open champions, yet—for substantial sums on two separate occasions. When I asked him about it, he said he didn't want to embarrass anybody and preferred not to mention it in the book—unless the players themselves said it was all right. They were contacted, and, no surprise, both vehemently opposed appearing in Crump's memoirs. I lobbied hard with Leon to name his two hall-of-fame victims, but he stood firm about respecting their wishes. (Anyone wishing to know their identity need only ask me.)

Among many of the people I talked with, the subject would often come up as to whether or not Leon Crump could have or should have played the PGA Tour. Such speculation tends to overlook what I, and several of Crump's friends and associates consider a stellar career in its own right. Man-to-man betting is legal in most of the South, where putting up one's bankroll on a test of skill is thought of as the most natural thing in the world. In some quarters, a gambling scratch golfer who risks his own cash is considered just as legitimate as the touring pro who plays for corporate monies. By these and any other standards, Leon Crump didn't fall to his lot; he rose to it.

JOHN STRAVINSKY
October 1996

An Early Score

In the summer of 1958, I was twenty-two, about half-broke, and stumbling through a marriage that wasn't working, when I took a little trip that would change my life.

I was employed as a machinist at the time, but my real talent was hitting a golf ball long and straight. The problem was, unless you were from a country club background or had a rich sponsor, there weren't many opportunities for a country boy to make a living beatin' a little white ball. To me, the game of golf just meant fun, distraction, and a supplemental income—that is, until the trip.

For several years now, I had seen sizable chunks of money changing hands out on the links around my hometown of Charlotte, North Carolina. I played hard and took down my share of bets, but never could accumulate much of a bankroll—I had a knack for handing back whatever I'd won and then some. As far as working in the machine shop, well, the pay wasn't bad, but I was always daydreaming about getting out into the open air and shooting the lights out in high-stakes matches, just like the rounders that hung out at the local golf courses—guys that never seemed to work a day in their lives.

One weekend, I played in some team matches against a few boys up from across the South Carolina border. Everyone except me was tossing around some pretty serious dough. I made up my mind that the first opportunity I had, I would get in on some of this action. One of the visitors, Bobby Howard, told me that anytime I wanted, I should come on down to Columbia, to the Sedgewood golf course, and I would guaranteed get a game. "Just make sure you bring plenty of cash," he told me with a wink, "in case you might lose."

About ten days later, I decided to get off work for a few days and head down to Columbia. Those boys had made out like bandits on their last trip through, and I figured that they couldn't have already spent all that money. My aim was to go down there and pick me up a few hundred, or maybe get lucky and win $1,000. That sure would be good pocket money to bring back. I was already a fearless golfer with a world of confidence. Unfortunately I didn't know much about managing my cash flow, especially when I didn't have any.

I knew that the hundred and change that I took with me wasn't much of a stake. Driving down in my '55 Ford Fairlane, I thought about how I should go about planning my opening moves. Should I just lay it all out, play nine holes for the hundred, then keep doubling up, or should I try and build up a roll by coming on like a nit at ten, twenty dollars?

When I got there, Howard, who I would play a lot down the road, didn't want to humor me with any nickel-and-dime stuff. He insisted on a fifty-dollar nassau right away. I asked around to see if anybody else wanted to play, but I couldn't get any takers—Howard must have touted them off. I had hoped to get to know the course first with a smaller bet, but Howard wouldn't go for it. So I agreed to fifty-dollars-a-side (front nine, back nine, and overall), that was fifty dollars more than I was holding, which of course I didn't let on.

The course threw me for a loop, especially the way the greens putted—they seemed to break against the grain uphill, which didn't make any sense to me. I lost the front side on the 9th hole by missing a five-footer, and wound up breaking even for the day by holing about the same length blood-tester on 18. I felt like I'd dodged a lot of bullets, but I really had no idea what I was supposed to do next.

It was getting dark when somebody suggested going to a nearby poolroom, and that was almost a relief to me. Dropping money on pool tables was nothing new. It seemed as good a place as any to part with what I had left in my pocket. Without the proper funds, I didn't see any future for me on that golf course. Anyway, I still had a half-tank of gas, which was all I needed to get back to Charlotte.

At the poolroom, I got jackpot, big-time lucky. Nobody had wanted to play any pool right off, which was fortunate since I would have blown my wad at the first offer of a ten-dollar nine-ball game. Anyway, I hadn't been there but fifteen minutes when a local bookie showed up looking for somebody to "pitch to the line" against. This I never expected. Pitching was one of my strong suits. I'd been a line-pitcher all my life, a world beater ever since the fourth grade when I was taking down regular lunch money pitchin' pennies.

This cat James was looking to pitch half-dollars at five-dollars-a-go, and I jumped on it like a hound on a pork chop. The room had oak floorboards which was just about my favorite surface. As a kid, I pitched on dirt, but once I got better at it, I learned to pitch on concrete and to make the coin land on its edge so it'll stop. It's the same thing on wood. You have to kind of spin it off of your fingers with the coin standing upright, and make sure that it doesn't land flat, or it will scoot. You could pitch any kind of coin, but half-dollars were my favorite; they had more weight and stopped so much easier. Right off I could see that James was an average pitcher. He was just lookin' for action, and without knowing it, falling into a major trap.

I worked my way ahead, slowly and surely. I didn't want to show too much early speed. At one point, while making change, James flashed the inside of his bankroll and my eyes about popped at seeing all the hundreds stuck in there. James felt that I was getting a lot of "lucky" stops, and I certainly didn't want to argue with him. He fancied himself to be a real pitchin' wizard, so I kept giving him the old line about how I'd "rather be lucky than good." About two in the morning, after some four hours of pitching, James up and quit me. I'd just about worn a groove in that line of chalk and James had lost $1,100 cash, the most green my pockets had ever seen.

I tiptoed out of that poolroom, drove a little ways, and checked into a motel down the road. I took a shower, stashed my cash under the pillow, and caught a few hours sleep. Then I headed back over to Sedgewood feeling like Superman. One of the first things I did at the course was take a golf cart out to the three finishing holes on each nine (I call them the "money" holes) and spent some time practice-putting and analyzing the breaks in detail. The grass was 328-grain

Bermuda, a tricky putting surface if you're not used to it. In effect, the ball did break a little uphill near where they had the cups cut. After a few practice putts, I had it down.

I caught up to Bobby Howard—he was a part-owner of the course—and a partner of his on the putting green. "Well, boys," I said, "I'm ready to play. Now I know the golf course, so let's roll." We started out playing at $100 a side, one-down automatic presses (additional double-up bets every time someone loses a hole).

The course was long and straight, about made to order for me. The 9th and 18th holes were par 5s, a big edge, since Bobby and the other guy weren't all that long off the tees. I won $1,800 from my opponents that second day and more than twice that much from the railbirds betting me on the side. It seemed like every next hole I played, people were popping out of the woods to bet against me and to back their local favorites. That was fine with me, because back then the sky was the limit, and my game was getting stronger with every dollar I won. Even James, the bookie, came out a few times to bet against me, which I looked upon as good luck. I lost a few times during the week, but never when he was on the other side. After four more days of play I had won the staggering sum of $31,000 playing golf. Bobby and all the locals had had enough.

Try to imagine what that kind of money was to a working stiff in 1958. As a machinist, I was pulling down about seventy-five dollars a week; after taxes, that adds up to $3,900 a year. That's only because I was lucky enough to get a top-paying grease job through a family connection. All I had ever wanted to do was play golf, and here I'd just about hit the damn lottery doin' it.

On the drive home I'd made up my mind that I would quit the working life—for then anyway. I wouldn't just walk out on my boss. After all, he'd been so good to me, letting me off work to play and all. I'd do it right; give notice and leave on good terms. After I went through my small fortune, I might need my job back. It's not like I wanted to be a professional touring golfer. No, I just figured that I'd live off of golf gambling for awhile and see how that went.

That was almost forty years ago. I haven't worked a day in my life since.

2

Caddy Days

Gambling is a way of life down South, not that I thought about it much. I just kind of grew into it.

In the spring of 1947, I started caddying at the Eastwood golf course, on the north side of Charlotte, up the street from where I went to school. I was twelve years old and didn't know the first thing about the game. To my family and the crowd of kids that I hung with, golf was considered a sissy sport mostly played by rich people—something we were not. I didn't feel one way or another about the game. All I knew was, carrying a golf bag for a nickel a hole, plus tips, sure beat the hell out of pushing a lawn mower at fifty cents a yard.

My daddy was in the taxi business; sometimes he owned and operated his cab, other times he worked for others. He and my mother never passed the third grade, and they never really pushed me in my schoolwork either. They scraped all their life and that's all they knew—that and going to church. When you are old enough, you go to work, this is what my parents expected of my brother Herbert and me. To them, earning money at the golf course seemed all right for a kid, but, of course, they never had any idea that I would start playing golf, much less gamble at it.

I soon discovered that everybody who caddied played a little golf—that's just the way it was. And the only way you played was for money. That was automatic; you just didn't think of turning down a bet, even if everybody was trying to steal your earnings. I was gambling at golf before I really knew how to swing a club. It was simple enough: hit the ball, go chase it, try and hit it a little better, go chase it again, and pay up when you lose.

Our caddy fee was forty-five cents, plus tips, and we usually wound up playing for most of it. We had these makeshift "caddylot" holes down at the bottom of a hill. They were about fifty or sixty yards apart, anywhere from three to five holes dug into the ground with sticks for flags. When we weren't carrying a bag, we were down there bumpin' heads, kicking up the dust at ten cents a hole, usually with one club that we passed around. On the golf course, the back nine had some holes hidden from the clubhouse, and we snuck out on those as much as possible. It was a whole new world to me, and even if I wasn't very good right at first, I had a great time at it. I loved the competition, and I got better, fast. "Why don't you play baseball like all the other kids?" my mother would ask me. Baseball never offered that much action.

There was an assistant pro, named Gum, who caddied with us sometimes. Gum was black and back then he could only play in the black tournaments, what they called the "chitlin' circuit." He had a beautiful swing and a soft touch, and he didn't mind robbing us regularly. Gum would hustle everybody. We were so thrilled to go out and play those holes on the back, we would have handed him our money, which is pretty much what we did anyway. He'd hustle everybody, play one of us for a dime, another for a quarter—he seemed to know exactly how much we had in our pockets. You could make three, four, even five dollars on a good day, and before you knew it, most of it would wind up in Gum's pocket.

One rainy day, a couple of us caddies were shooting dice for a nickel a throw with Leroy, who ran the club's kitchen. It was one of those days when I got really lucky and won everybody's money. I was just taking down the last bit of change from Leroy's cash register, when the Tru-Ade delivery man drove up. Tru-Ade was all right—we'd trade him found golf balls for orange drinks. Anyway, he jumped in the craps game, and next thing you know I'd won all his route money, and he was trying to get me to roll for a case of drinks off of his truck. Since I really had no use for the drinks, I pulled up and headed for home whistling like a catbird. When I got to our house, on what they called the "Mill Hill," I saw my Uncle Henry who was always ribbing me. On this day, for some reason he decided to see how much money I had on me. He was playing around, digging in my pockets, when he realized they were filled with quarters and loose dollar bills. He and my mother immediately wanted to know where I'd come up with what was around forty dollars, and, I guess, looked like a lot more. I was thirteen years old, and it was the most money I'd ever had.

"I made it caddyin'," I told them.

"You don't make that much money caddyin'," she said.

"Well, I've been saving it," I lied.

"All in change, in your pockets? For lyin' to me, you can see me in the back room," she said.

I knew that I was about to get a whuppin'—my first in a long time, and the last I would ever get from my mother. She started beating on me with a belt and said she was gonna' beat on me until I told her where I got the money from. You didn't talk back to Momma, so like an idiot, I told her that I won it shooting dice. This was probably the worst thing I could have said to a devout, church-going Baptist. She beat me some more while I covered up, until she must have gotten tired. Momma made me promise not do it anymore, and I said I wouldn't.

When my daddy got home, he thought it was all kind of funny. But from that day on, I was careful to keep my bad habits to myself. I never let on until many years later that I played golf for money. Even at twenty-one, my mother would have beaten me with that belt all over again. So I kept everything quiet.

Meanwhile, that big win with the dice was kind of a turning point. Carrying all that money around—forty dollars was a lot for a kid then—seemed to relax me and give me confidence in my little golf bets. At the same time I was practicing and getting better. I would take a club home with me, get up every day at the crack of dawn, and go beat the ball in a near-by field. I made up my own little "course" with sticks and dug-up holes, and nobody could see me getting better. It was a great feeling to know that I was talented at something, and of course, the most immediate way to prove it was to take down some dough off of my co-workers.

*   *   *

When I first started betting with Gum and the other caddies, everybody was spotting me strokes, even on those little caddylot holes. But you had to learn how to handicap yourself compared to others, or your ass was had. It seemed like overnight, Gum was refusing to spot me anymore—he was still beating me, it was just a lot closer—and I was giving the other boys strokes. As far back as I can remember, I was relaxed playing for any sum of money, which gave me a big edge. It just didn't matter how much was at stake, since I never put much mind to it. While my game would pick up a little bit at the prospect of winning some extra change, others would suffer from the pressure of possibly losing their earnings. I never put a premium on money—never did, and, I guess, I never will.

When we weren't playing each other, all of us caddies would bet on the guys we were carrying for. My man against your man for a quarter—that sort of thing. You had to stay sharp and pay attention to everybody's game, which I did anyway. It was a point of pride—"my man is better than your man," or "I can help my guy better than you can help yours." You always had these thoughts. People didn't deal too much in handicaps back then, but after a year of caddying, I could pretty much figure out what all the golfers around Eastwood could be expected to shoot on any given day. I knew the long hitters, the wild hitters, the good and bad putters, the sandbaggers, the moaners, the losers, and the winners. Most of all, I watched to see how much money different golfers were playing for, knowing all the time how it would affect their games.

Betting against other caddies could be treacherous. There was one character, about five years older than me, who was often in cahoots with his man. I didn't want any part of that action. He would get a nice, fat tip for stomping another player's ball down into the ground, and his own player always seemed to have a perfect lie, even when playing from the rough. Sometimes, the caddy would ask his man if he could share a piece of his action. If a guy was betting twenty dollars, the caddy would take five of it, which, by helping his man cheat, he was sure not to lose.

As I got older, sometimes I'd offer to play a couple of holes against the man I was caddying for. This wouldn't do at a country club, but Eastwood was a down-to-earth place. You had to know your player before you would make such an offer. Also, you would only lay it out if you had an action man who was playing by himself. Otherwise, you ran the risk of embarrassing somebody, in which case you, the caddy, would be gone. I would get to the 5th or 6th hole—again, far enough away from the clubhouse—and ask my man if he wouldn't go one hole, double-or-nothing, for my caddy fee, letting me use his clubs, of course.

Golfers, especially working men, had a lot of respect for the playing ability of caddies back then. There were a lot of takers on that offer, and I think most of them liked the challenge—that and the thought that they might get a free carry out of it. Everybody's always lookin' for something for nothing. Right there's the ruin of a lot of gamblers. On my end, once again, I just didn't care; I knew I was going to be out there anyway, and if I had to carry a bag for free for a couple of more hours—so be it. I knew deep inside that I was always the favorite and not just based on my rising abilities. You see, ego would make the golfer accept the bet, and pride would get in his way, since he damn sure didn't want to lose to his caddy. I understand that touring pro Peter Jacobsen often lets his regular caddy play other pros one par-3 hole for twenty dollars during a practice round, and the caddy hardly ever loses.

When I was about fifteen, I made the play with a lawyer named Charlie Donnally who I had caddied for a few times. He was a big man, didn't talk much, but I knew he usually bet high with others, so I figured playing alone, he might like a little action. I waited until the 6th tee and made my double-or-nothin' pitch. Charlie thought about it for a minute, and said "all right." After snap-hooking his ball near the out-of-bounds, he handed me his driver. I'll never forget that club; it was a beautiful, lacquered, Tommy Armour model that was treated so nice it looked like it'd never been hit. I couldn't wait to crack one out there.

Maybe I over-swung, maybe I looked up—I can't remember. What comes back, clear as yesterday, was the way I swung down at the ball, hitting behind it about six inches, into the ground, hard. That shaft split right in two—like I'd hacked it on the hosel with a pole ax.

"You're going to have to pay for that club, son," was all Charlie said. There were few repair people around in those days, so they had to send it back to the factory. But Charlie didn't care to wait, so he bought another club which I paid for. It cost the equivalent of a week's solid caddying. Needless to say, our little match ended on my faulty swing. That was the first and last hole I ever played with Charlie.

Around the time when I learned to play, many of your best golfers came from the caddy yards. I'm thankful for the experience because it's surely the only way I ever would have picked up the game. More than that, caddying taught me to use the "peepers"—to learn by watching. I didn't realize it at the time, but every idle moment spent lugging somebody's sticks was time used for picking up the finer points.

I learned to judge people by their golf swings and picked up those swings I liked best. Watching the bad player, I'd figure out what exactly he was doing wrong to mess up his shots; then I'd watch the good player and visualize what I would be like hitting the ball the way he did. Caddies did a lot of waiting around, and I always had a club in my hand, chipping around to an imaginary hole, just getting a feel.

I noticed that Gum addressed his ball with the blade wide open, just the opposite of "hooding" the club. Somehow I came to copy that; this allowed me to compensate for my strong hook swing. I've gotten more squared up over the years, but when I was learning, I loved the feel of having that clubhead open. Years later, Gum would sometimes caddy for me, and he would remind me to "open her up" anytime I'd start to get off-line to the left.

In those days, people played by eye, they didn't play by distance. It wouldn't take me but three or four holes of watching my man before I'd know what to tell him to hit. Before I became so nearsighted, I could judge distance pretty well and club people accordingly. Nobody played from yardage; you just visualized the shot and figured, well, this looks like a six-iron, seven-iron, whatever. You'd also go by what he'd hit in his previous rounds and have your landmarks—that bush is a six-iron for this golfer, that tree is a four for that golfer. I can't remember exactly when the 150-yard markers came in, but when I started, we judged distance by sight, feel, and memory.

One time I was caddying across town at the Carolina golf course for a detective named Al Ramsey. He was a hothead, but a good golfer who hit a long ball. He had faith in me, but I really didn't know the layout all that well. On this particular day, he was playing a beer distributor for a couple hundred, all even coming down the 18th. He laid out a fine drive, which left him with a shot over a lake to a tabletop green. He asked me what I thought. I thought, well, I sure don't want to get him wet. So, I told him four-wood, which he went and sailed some thirty, forty yards past the green. The shot cost him the cheese, and he was steamed enough not to leave me any tip. It woke me up to the importance of clubbing. From that day I made sure I knew the approach shot distances—at least on the money holes.

Probably the biggest day I had caddying was a drizzly afternoon when I had cut school and there weren't any other boys around. A foursome wanted to go out with these huge leather bags, big enough to pack a side of beef in. Back then, nobody paid any attention to the fourteen-club rule; if a guy needed five wedges and three five-woods, he'd take them, even if his boy could hardly lift the bag. These fellas knew I couldn't begin to tote all their clubs, so they suggested choosing a selection and stashing them into two bags. I would carry one bag on each shoulder down the middle of the fairway. I did that for thirty-six holes and nearly dropped when it was over.

One of the big talkers in the group was a golf hustler and con artist named Charlie Simpson. Charlie had a good day and gave me a big tip. I remember thinking this cat's all right; I liked his style. I'm sure he didn't think all that much about me, but within a few more years, he would have his hands full trying to beat his former caddy. Charlie didn't book too many losers; I didn't either.

3

An Outdoor Poolroom

Fate must have delivered me to Eastwood, where I got my real education. The golf course is located in a run-down neighborhood off the corner of The Plaza and Eastway Avenue. It's fitting, really, since Eastwood has always been a blue collar, hard knocks golf course—the equivalent of an outdoor poolroom. With all the cash that changed hands there, it sometimes seemed like an open-air casino.

Don't get me wrong. Today, it's a nice track where all kinds of people can play golf for a reasonable price. The greens are small, well-groomed, and the hardscrabble terrain is plenty challenging, especially for those playing it the first time. In its heyday, say 1955 to 1970, Eastwood was a unique golf-gambler's paradise—action central all the way. There's no scene like it anymore; if there is, I wish somebody'd let me know about it so I could go there right now.

At sixteen, I quit high school and landed a good job as a machinist at a tool and die shop. There I started as a general operator building machines and making tools. I like to think that it gave my hands a feel for golf, but it was nerve-racking precision work. We made parts for aircraft. When I'd make a die for mass production, I'd be working within thousandths of an inch. It was tedious labor, but then I wasn't much for work anyhow—by the time I was nineteen, my mind was usually out at Eastwood thinking about what I might be missing.

After taking a steady job, I pretty much quit caddying and focused all my efforts on playing. Clayton Heafner, the legendary pro who owned Eastwood—he finished second in the U.S. Open twice in three years ('49-'51)—once told my brother, "If he starts playing golf every day instead of working, he could be one great player." That kind of stuck in the back of my mind and made me want to play all the time—by that I mean all day, instead of just every day.

As far as golf schooling goes, I'm pretty much self-taught—I never was too much on lessons. When I began playing so much, practice seemed to be a waste of time. I might hit a few balls to work on some part of my game, but not if it interfered with even the remotest possibility of a game. Again, there was Heafner again, whose every word was gospel to me. "Don't let anybody mess you up," he told me. "Just keep what you got and play."

Eventually, I changed machine shops and wound up working for a boss who liked golf and understood I needed more time to play. I'd get off at three in the afternoon, and from spring to fall I'd be at the golf course until after dark. They called me "Greasy Man" back then, since I never bothered to go home to wash and change. My work clothes would be covered with oil, but I just went straight from the parking lot to the first tee. I played whoever wanted to play and it seemed like there was always a money game. It was only a matter of time before I'd leave the working life behind.

*   *   *

Eastwood was so convenient—well inside the city limits. At the time, there were only four public golf courses in Charlotte, and two of them were only nine holes. All the action guys would hurry out to Eastwood after work knowing they could get a game there for just about any amount of money they wanted. People gathered in the clubhouse because there was always something going on. It didn't matter if it was bad weather. If it was pouring down rain, we might make a "cross-country" bet for fifty or a hundred dollars, on how many strokes it would take me (or anybody else) to get from the 1st tee to the 15th hole. It was a zigzag 1,000-or-so yards across separate fairways, over a pond, and a creek. I'd usually bet that I could do it in six, but if I missed one shot the slightest bit, I was dead in the water. One time I won a bundle making it in five when I didn't need to; I was only trying to lag my putt, and it went in. After that, I couldn't get a cross-country bet for months.

When it snowed, we'd paint the golf balls red and play. We made little troughs on the green for putting. Sometimes we would putt an obstacle course through the pro shop into a cup positioned in the locker room. Seemed like bad weather brought out a lot of grudge match stuff. It didn't matter if it was you or somebody else golfing—you just wanted to bet or play.

One day in March, in the early '60s, it was raining buckets and the course was half under water. I didn't really want to get soaked, but one thing led to another and I wound up making a $300 bet with a bookie named Stuart Bragg that I could go out right then and shoot one over par on the front side, the easier nine holes. The deal was that I would have to play the ball "flat," meaning I couldn't improve my lies, except I wouldn't have to putt through water on the greens.

As I was standing on the first tee, I could feel the rain let up a little. Still, I made sure I lined my drive out toward the right side, away from the low spots on the left where water tended to accumulate. By the time I got to my ball, the rain had all but stopped and the sun was starting to peek through. "My God," said Bragg, who was riding along with an umbrella, "you called the damn weather bureau. You knew this was gonna' happen."

Well, I hadn't, although I did have a feeling the weather might change. Anyway, I birdied the 1st hole, parred the next three, and birdied the 5th. I was getting ready to tee off on the 6th, an easy par 5, when Bragg said, "Let's go in. I don't need to sit here and watch you steal my money." He peeled me off three bills from his bankroll, and I never had to finish the nine.

Bragg was one of the main characters in a cast of regulars out at Eastwood. Like almost everybody else, he was looking for an edge, but he was also an all-around good ole' boy. When it came to betting me, didn't matter what it was, he always seemed to get the worst of it. I'll never forget a bet I made with Horace "Catfish" Phillips, a good friend who liked to start up with me whenever things got a little slow. My problem has always been that I'll take the worst of it just to get in the action. If I can't get a golf game, I'm liable to take five-to-one that I can climb the Matterhorn in penny loafers.

On this particular day, Catfish had bet me $500 that I couldn't shoot 30 on the back nine, playing three balls. In other words, it was as if I was playing each hole three times, and I would get to keep my best score. Anyway, on the par-4 15th, I had missed the green with the first two of my approach shots and was only one under (30 was six under par). Far as I was concerned, that money was gone. It was at this point that Bragg strolled over to Catfish and accused him of out-and-out robbery.

"Now Bragg," Catfish said, "don't make no difference what kind of bet you make with Leon, you don't necessarily have to win it, no matter how good it sounds in the clubhouse."

"That right?" said Bragg. "Well if you don't think you got the best of it, I'll give you $475 right now for your bet."

"Sold—give me the money," Catfish said.

In other words, Bragg was buying the bet, under the assumption that I was not going to shoot five under par on the last four holes, which I would have to start with by getting up-and-down from a hundred yards on my remaining ball on this hole. Well, I heard what was going down, and I'd be lying if I didn't say it pumped me up. In those days, I fired at the pin all the time—still do pretty much—and I had probably by then already shot 30 a half-dozen times just playing one ball alone, much less getting to pick my best out of three.

So, I knocked my shot up on the green and rolled in a tricky ten-foot, side-hill putt. I birdied the next two holes, putting me four under. Then on the par-5 18th, I caught a four-iron dead perfect to about three feet for my eagle putt and, lordy, lordy, I had shot my 30. I caught up to Bragg in the clubhouse and told him to pay me. He seemed confused.

"I already paid Catfish," he said.

"No, you *bought* the bet from Catfish," I reminded him. "You haven't *paid* anybody yet."

21

"Godawmighty, Crump, you don't think I'd put up $975 just to try and win $25, do you?" Bragg said.

"Well that's what you done done," I said.

Bragg paid, but he didn't like it. The next day, he was still walking around mumbling something about how he couldn't possibly have made such a dumb-ass bet. It turns out he was trying to pick up a quick, safe, four percent on his money. Really, with four holes left, how are you going to shoot five under? Except I somehow did at that time. I guess sometimes you feel like you can birdie every hole, and you actually can.

On good days, there were anywhere from twenty to forty golfers looking for a bet at Eastwood. Clayton Heafner called it "doin' somethin'." "Ain't anybody around here gonna' do somethin'?" he would ask until somebody did, whether it was craps, bumper pool (there was a little table in the back), or a straight-up golf game. You could pick out whoever you wanted to match up with for twenty-five, fifty, or a hundred dollars and just go out and play. Sometimes the games got bigger depending on how much ribbing went on before they got to the tees. There was always a lot of ego involved.

There was no shortage of colorful characters out at Eastwood. Charlie Simpson was a stone-cold con artist who took up the game in his thirties and could beat almost any living human on the planet; the idea was to stay clear of him when he drank. Cut-Shot Jerret was a big, burly plumbing contractor who could hit a sand wedge off of concrete and stop the ball on a dime. Crazy Cole couldn't play too much but would crack us up with stuff like, "Where I am, is where

I'm at." Scoop Jennings could putt the lights out—his ball would disappear into the hole like a rabbit—but he never seemed to win. Bob Bryant (more on him later) was my personal rival and a cutthroat son-of-a-bitch—between us, we must have shot thirty rounds under 65 at an average of $1,000 a pop. Gastonia Greg played with a hunk of wood stuck under his golf shoe for a month (he thought he was correcting a stance problem) until he ruined his back. It was a crazy crew, and if you didn't see some nut case for a couple of months, or even a year, there'd be another to take his place.

Sometimes we would close out Eastwood in the dusky-dark and take our play out to Paradise Valley, a par-3 course with lights. The shadows from the lights bothered me a lot and oftentimes would get me to shanking the ball, but there were too many games out there to pass up. Bragg was the worst; he'd be stuck serious money over at Eastwood, then try and get out by dragging you over to the par 3, where his wife worked—he'd have her there until all hours of the morning, keeping the place open for his action. At this particular course, they had two cups cut into every green; you'd change the flagstick to the other hole each time after putting, to save wear on the surface. This made for a natural handicap that Bragg thought up; I would allow him to putt to whatever hole he landed nearest to. Funny thing was, he'd try to hit it in the middle to get lucky and have a close pick, but often he'd manage to miss the green entirely.

Even though the holes were only about seventy to ninety yards long, Bragg tooled around the place in an electric cart and wouldn't give anybody a ride. It was kind of a joke, with the layout maybe a total 500 yards square. He considered this a big edge, driving around with his two clubs—we only used

23

wedge and putter—while we'd be hoofing it. Actually, you would get tired after about fifty holes, since the 7th, 8th, and 9th holes were a little uphill. But you'd play as fast as you could play, going round, and round, and round, like a rat on a wheel. Many was the time we played through the night, only to hit Eastwood when they reopened in the morning.

One time Charlie Simpson was looking to head over to Paradise with Catfish, who was a strong par-3 man. Now, Catfish had had a few beers at Eastwood that day, so Charlie figured he was getting in on something easy. Charlie was what we call a good "manager," a guy who was very careful with his pocket money. But Catfish ended up scalding Charlie for around $700 or $800 that night, and Charlie got hot.

"I thought you was drunk," he yelled at Catfish. "You trapped me."

"I didn't tell you I was drunk," said Catfish. "You trapped yourself."

Two weeks later, Charlie was still steamed and wanted a piece of Catfish. When Catfish told him he had to go in to work at the fire department that night, Charlie offered him his shift's pay, up front, to play. Catfish took it and knocked him off again, this time for around $1,500. "I like this," he said after Charlie paid him off. "Two paychecks is my idea of a good job."

There were all kinds of games at Eastwood. It seemed like no two people ever played the same way twice. One time there was a group of players who wouldn't trust each other and decided against playing the "leaf rule." Now the leaf rule is common in the fall, when a ball can easily roll under falling leaves. You generally play drop another ball, no penalty, if it's landed around leaves and you can't find it. But these guys felt the rule would be abused, so they decided to play that you *must find your ball at all times.*

Anyway, near the woods on the 16th hole, one of the players located his ball surrounded by fallen maple leaves. He knew he wasn't allowed to move it, and he wanted to get rid of the obstructions for a clean hit, so he took a match to the leaves. They got to crackling and burning away, but once they got going good, the cover on his balata golf ball also began to melt. Within minutes, it was a gooey mess, with the inner rubber wound coming apart all over the place. Once the fire burned out, the others made him play that ball, or what was left of it, and he somehow chipped the mangled thing onto the green. Insisting on rules, they broke his chops by making him hole out with his "original ball." He might as well have been putting a half-burnt charcoal briquette. Of course he lost the hole.

One thing for sure—once you went through Eastwood you were ready to play anywhere, and I'm not talking only about course conditions. At Eastwood you got an education and game experience, so to speak; you learned how to take care of yourself. A lot of hustlers came through here because they'd heard about all the action, but few of them ever left town with any money.

Another thing about Eastwood. There was no driving range there, but after playing every shot in the world off every kind of surface—hard dirt, grass, clay, whatever—to really small greens, you learned to play an all-around game. People think you have to hit a zillion practice shots to become a scratch player, but you don't really when you're playing all the time. When I first traveled to other courses, the greens seemed as big as acre lots and impossible to miss; firing at the flagsticks was like shootin' darts. There was no sprinkler system at Eastwood and very little watering, which meant that you learned to play off hardpan and scrub grass; that made it all the easier when you'd go play a course with lush fairways where the ball would be sitting up like an apple on a teacup.

Nowadays, on most courses, players who like to play for a little something are lucky if they can get a three-dollar nassau. Try to ask somebody to bet a sawbuck and they'll look at you like you're Nick the Greek or Fast Eddie. There was a time at Eastwood when even the caddies wouldn't bet less than ten dollars. Players would sometimes jaw and jabber for hours trying to make a game, careful not to fall out of line. They knew one wrong move, one "tell-you-what-I'm-gonna'-do," that didn't add up and everybody would jump on the sucker like fleas on a hound. Usually somebody came up with an offer that sounded good to somebody else, and everybody would make bets. Sometimes the match would go off a foursome, a fivesome, or even a sixsome, with ten or fifteen carts tagging along and everybody gambling on every hole. There would be thousands of dollars bet, mostly among people riding and watching. It was quite a place.

There came a point where I spent most of my waking hours at Eastwood. I quit my job, quite simply because I didn't have enough time to play golf. I was also losing too many players to other golfers just because I had to go to work. Say I broke even with a guy one afternoon playing until dark; the logical thing would be to pick up the next morning where we'd left off and put the balls back up in the air. I couldn't do that until I decided to trade in my day job. Of course, I wouldn't have done it if I didn't have absolute faith that I could always support myself and my family—and I always have.

On weekends, most players would go find other courses, and we would leave Eastwood to the Sunday players. But come Monday morning, everybody would be back looking for a game. There were so many good players, too—players that in this day and age would be concentrating on trying to make the pro tour. But in the late '50s, they were thinking more of their action games than anything else. Weekday golf has pretty much carried over for me to this day—I don't really play golf on weekends. You generally find your best games during the week. That's the "job" aspect of being a golf hustler.

4

A Hustler's Teachers

Even if you're just going to be a golf hustler, you've got to have some guidance along the way. I guess with all my natural talent I might have made it on the golf tour if the right people had steered me differently. But I'm very lucky for having spent some quality time around two of the greatest and orneriest golfers of their day, Clayton Heafner and Tommy Bolt. They were important influences on me, not just in showing me how to hit the ball, but also in an area that's harder to define—how to approach the game mentally and how to respect what you're doing out on the course. They were classy, proud golfers from another era, and I'd like to feel that some of that rubbed off on me.

Looking in a whole other direction, I learned a lot from my days spent around Titanic Thompson, the greatest all-around hustler that ever lived. It would be impossible to learn and pull off all of the cons and scams Titanic had going, but hanging with him definitely taught me not to be a sucker. Titanic showed me that you can be an outlaw and still be successful.

*   *   *

"Heaf" was born about thirty years too early to really cash in on pro golf. Still, he still did fairly well and was probably the third or fourth highest money winner in the late '40s. But that added up to about only $15,000 to 20,000 a year— peanuts compared to today's handouts. When a group of businessmen bought some farmland and built Eastwood in 1949, they brought in Heafner, a "name" pro, for a ten percent share. He ran the joint when he wasn't out on the tour, and bit-by-bit he got to be a majority owner by buying out the others or even picking up some shares through gambling winnings. One of the slices came from a supermarket chain owner who played decent enough golf but wasn't any match for Heaf. Another piece came from an investor who made the mistake of calling Heaf and asking for a monthly return. "Until you come in here and make hot dogs like we do," Heaf told the guy, "the course will not make one nickel in profit. We'll have gold-plated flagpoles out here before it does." The man sold his share to Heaf the following week.

Heafner was an all-around gambler, but I know he made buckets of money playing gin rummy on the tour. Sometimes it seemed that was all that he felt the tour was good for, that and hustling golf. He took South African Bobby Locke as a partner and they barbecued every top player there was back then. His temper was legendary and he was famous for pulling out of tournaments. I don't think he cared all that much for tournament golf.

There was a famous photograph taken of him playing out of a tree at Riviera in the L.A. Open. The following year, at that same tournament, he was introduced—on the first tee— by an announcer who pronounced his name wrong, said that he was from Linnville, North Carolina, and added that he hoped "Heefner" wouldn't have so much trouble with the trees this time around. Heaf walked over to him and said, "Look here, buddy. My name's 'Heafner,' not 'Heefner.' I'm from Charlotte, not Linnville, and as far as your goddam trees, I'm not gonna be in them 'cause I'm leavin' right now." He got into his car and took off.

Heafner didn't like many people; he was pretty gruff and let you know it if he didn't want you around. When he returned to Eastwood after losing the 1951 U.S. Open, by one stroke to Ben Hogan, he hit the bottle pretty good. Seems like I was one of the few people that he could tolerate having around. When he wanted to hit balls, I would watch, then I would go shag them. A few years later, my game had improved enough that I could play with him. There were many times I got the best of him for a hundred or for whatever we were playing. But there was something off about it; he never would really bear down against me like he did against other people. Of course, beating him pumped me up pretty good. Far as I was concerned, finishing second in the Open was just as good as winning it. So it was like I was beating the Open winner—hell, now I could play with anybody.

When he wanted to, Heaf could kill you with the wedge; I picked that up mostly from him. I swear my eyes were glued to his hands whenever he played any chip shot; I knew ahead of time that the ball was going to wind up inside two feet from the cup. I wanted to know how he got it there. From what I could see, he moved the ball back in his stance, locked his wrists completely down, closed the clubface, and it would take off low. It looked like he skulled the ball. It would hit the green, take one hop, and slam on the brakes just like the Roadrunner. Then you'd see him hit what looked like the same shot completely different; the ball would land a little shorter and roll its way up to the hole. It was all in the hands and wrists.

Heafner didn't talk much, but if a picture's worth a thousand words, I've got an encyclopedia's worth just watching his smooth, repetitive swing. He was a big man with a soft touch and great tempo. As far as his temper went, I never did see it out on the golf course. Early on, I was quite a hothead myself, but I would never show anything when I played with Heaf. Here was a man with a terrible temper, exercising total self-control while out on the course. If he could do it I could too. He taught me the value of serious golf—I call it golf with a focus.

Sometime in the early '60s, I was down at the Cape Fear golf club in Wilmington, North Carolina, trying to qualify for an amateur tournament when I met "Terrible" Tommy Bolt. Now here's a case where a reputation can be totally wrong. Tommy Thunder, or whatever other nickname he went by, is best known for his temper, but he's actually one of the nicest, warmest individuals you'll ever meet. Most people choose to remember him for the time he threw his driver into the drink at the 1960 U.S. Open at Cherry Hills, in Denver. It's unfortunate that the public overlooks the fact that he won the Open over Gary Player (by five strokes) at Southern Hills in Tulsa two years earlier.

Anyway, Tommy always enjoyed a good match, and we must have bumped heads a hundred times over a five-year span. "Don't try and hustle a hustler," he used to tell me, and I swear I never did try. All I wanted to do was play the best, which he was.

The first time we ever played, down at Bardmore in Largo, Florida, Tommy beat me, one up on the front nine. I think we were playing for $200, something like that, and I caught a whiff of his temperament—not his temper, but his temperament. We were standing up on the 10th tee, and I told him I would "press" the back nine (double the bet).

"You can't press me," he snarled like a bulldog. "I'm Tommy Bolt." I told him I'd press anyway and he damned well better take the bet if he wanted anymore of my action. Around the 16th hole, he was now down two holes when he spoke up, "I'll press you."

"You can't press me," I fired back. "I'm Leon Crump."

Of course, I couldn't keep a straight face and Tommy just stood there with his head cocked trying to figure out what he had.

"Damn, boy," he told me. "I guess you're my kind of people."

We flip-flopped, back and forth when we played; most of the games were staked by Lloyd Farentino, a sporting type who liked to back us both and threw other partners in the mix. So neither one of us ever dropped very much of his own money against each other.

Tommy was the best wind player I ever saw, and like Clayton, he was tops with the wedge. He could land the ball so softly on the green, it was amazing; he used to claim he could plop a ball into a lake and not leave a ripple—that's how soft he hit it. You take a guy like Greg Norman. Great talent, but even he can only hit a wedge one way—full out. Bolt and a few old-time players like him could hit dozens of variations on the shot: cut it, stop it, float it, feather it, knock it down—and that's just the wedge shots. Hell, Bolt could *draw*, or even *hook* a wedge shot from forty feet away.

Against the wind, he could what I call "hold" it, when the breeze was coming right to left, and he'd just cut it into the wind and stop it at the flag. Same thing if it was blowing the other way, just the reverse, hook or draw it. And he was quite a con man, too. Sometimes he'd hit a three-iron into a fierce wind and hit it high when you'd think he would knock it down. The next time he had near the same shot, he'd hit a nine-iron low and make it look like a three—he'd always show you the club to get you all screwed up. The best thing to do was to ignore what club he hit—'cause you couldn't duplicate it anyway—and just try to copy the smooth, effortless swing. He could work the ball anyway he wanted to work it.

Tommy tried to get me out on the pro tour and I know he was disappointed that I never got there. He was like a father to me and once offered to sponsor me, but it was just never meant to be. He even loaned me money a few times. Most of all, he'd help me with my game, which is really unheard of when you're gambling with somebody. He gave me confidence about my driving, which often tended towards the wild. "Go on and try and hit that long ball," he would say. "That'll set you up mentally, take pressure off you."

I guess that's one of the things that I took from Tommy. He showed me you can like somebody and still try and beat the pants off them—especially when it comes to money games. He was a fierce competitor on tour, but he was a super-determined one-on-one player. As Tommy would tell me, "You gotta be proud to play this game. Whoever you're playin', you got to get out there and show 'em they can't beat you."

Titanic Thompson had been a gambling legend for a half-century by the time I met him in 1964. I guess with all the action we had going at Eastwood, it was only natural that he would turn up in Charlotte, since it was his business to know where the money games were being played. I had heard so many stories about his proposition bets over the years and the wild scores he had made across the country that there was one I just had to bring up right away. Supposedly, Titanic had once won a bundle from a mark by betting that he could successfully throw an ordinary key into a keyhole from across a room.

When "Ti" first walked into the Eastwood clubhouse on that springy-wintry day, I jumped up and introduced myself, told him that he could bust me right then and there with the keyhole bet. I pulled out a roll of cash, got the key from the register, and pointed to the front door lock. He just laughed and said that a long time ago in his travels, he'd beaten an oil-man out of some money by throwing a key in the correct slot of an old-time hotel key-box behind the front desk. Apparently, enough people were there, and the story grew like Paul Bunyan's ox. Legends do tend to stretch out a bit, but I can say that even in his seventies, Titanic Thompson could hoodwink you like Houdini.

For most of his life, Ti had been a scratch golfer playing either right- or left-handed, a 200-average bowler the same way, a crack pistol shooter, a champion horseshoes thrower, a world-class penny pitcher, a cold-blooded cardsharp, and all that's just for starters. There wasn't a game he couldn't play, and people were attracted to him like moths to a flame. Now that he was gettin' on in age, maybe he didn't match up in the games so well—except cards, where he could mark or stack the deck, deal seconds however he liked—but he could still hustle like nobody else. Suckers would line up beggin' to get trapped, especially when he flashed that big bankroll, with $1,000 bills in it. I actually saw fools play poker with him, which was nothing but sheer charity.

Ti lit up the scene like a Christmas tree. Out at Paradise Valley one day, he was trying to unload some big old Zircon imitation diamond which nobody would go for. Next thing you know, he was borrowing a pistol from behind the counter and had conned somebody into betting him $200 he couldn't hit a quarter thrown in the air from twenty-five feet. He did, of course—right through the center—but I think he could have hit a dime from fifty feet. Ti once told me that he liked to get the odds at least 9–1 in his favor when he was betting. At the same time, he would tell people in that lazy Texas drawl of his, "I just loo-oove to gamble." Hell, he loved to steal.

Another time, he bet us that he could out-distance any drive by throwing a golf ball in the air and blasting it with a twelve-gauge. Here again, you've got to bet it to sweat it, and we did. I popped one out about 300-and-change, and he got up there with that serious look, flipped whitey up in the air, and blasted that sucker to the next county. Now, I thought for sure that we would find the remains of a pulverized golf ball close by. But Ti got himself a search party, and they came up with the ball, a marked Titleist, about 600 yards away—half-shredded and riddled with shot.

Flipping cards was another of Ti's tricks. He could take a playing card, flick it sideways and make it stick in a watermelon fifty feet away. I tried it and couldn't get the card to go five feet; he would bet on twenty tries, and do it on, say, the eighteenth try, when you knew he was laying down all along. Anything he offered to bet on, you knew he could do it in one try.

Before Titanic came to town, he sent around Greg Stevens, a top pool player, to try to trap me with the fifteen numbered balls. They had heard that I was live bait around the tables, which was true. Problem was, Greg was just as live around the golf course as I was in the poolroom. We played some marathon sessions—all night in pool, all day in golf, and we pretty much broke even, which didn't please Ti too much. Ti hated expenses, he called it, "gettin' beat by the knife and fork."

One day, I was going against another golfer Ti had brought up, a Texas state amateur champion. We were playing a wedge-and-putter match, playing the wedges from the tees. We were dead-even late in the round, and I knew I'd better get going. So I hit my drive with the putter, smacked it about 230, 240 yards, picked up a birdie on that hole and never looked back. "Son," said Ti, "when I head back out on the road, you're goin' with me."

At the time, Ti didn't play much golf anymore—he mostly liked to stake good players. That was his way most of his life; if he personally couldn't beat somebody, he'd find somebody who could. One time he had a big-money checkers game against a top player. Ti put a champion player behind a peek-hole in the ceiling, an expert who signaled him the moves through a "thumper" wired to Ti's leg. Once we went on the road together, there was no escaping his attempts to lock me up. At breakfast in a coffee shop, he'd get that sly grin and say, "Hey, how much do you think that waitress weighs?" No way would I touch a setup like that.

In his prime, Ti was said to be equal to anybody in the world at golf. In Los Angeles, he shellacked George Von Elm, the 1926 U.S. Amateur champion, who had just beaten Bobby Jones. A favorite routine of his as he got older was to beat a sucker out of a few hundred in a round of golf and make it look real lucky by controlling slices and skulled shots. When the sucker started beefing about the outcome, Ti would turn on him kind of mean. "Your game is nothin', buddy. Hell, I'd bet $5,000 right now I can beat you playing lefty." The player would jump at that, and would of course lose, since Ti was a natural left-hander.

One of the most famous golf hustles he had was in Chicago, betting he could drive a ball 600 yards. What he did was tee it up over frozen Lake Michigan; he gave it a good whack and the ball rolled near a half-mile. For another setup, he would ask a maintenance man to water a green down real good. Then he'd lay a heavy hose down, run it up to the cup and leave it there overnight. The next day, he'd be playing the hole and ask for 3–1 odds that he could knock in a thirty-foot putt. Of course the putt was on the line of that watering hose, and all he had to do was run the ball down into that invisible rut and it would track right into the hole.

He took a Charlotte golfer named Frank Stone on the road to Texas with him and according to Frank, they pulled off the old caddy con. Ti had Frank, a scratch golfer, buy some old overalls—Frank normally dressed like Doug Sanders with matching purple pants and shoes, stuff like that—and sent him out ahead of time to get a job caddying at a course where Ti had been struggling to beat the club champ. Frank caddied for a few days, then one day Ti showed up at the caddylot and asked to pick out his own caddy. He selected Frank who caddied for him as he went back and forth over a few rounds with their intended victim.

The guy was tough as nails and wouldn't give up any strokes. Ti couldn't maneuver him, so finally he let him have it in the clubhouse. "You ain't got one nickel of gamble in you," he told him. "Hell, I'll bet you wouldn't even play my caddy unless he gave you strokes." He went on and on for awhile, then turned to Frank and said "Boy, you play any golf?" Frank said he played a little, and Ti turned around and asked the opponent if he'd play the caddy. Being club champ, he could hardly turn it down and the match was arranged for $5,000.

Ti told Frank not to play flat out, just beat him enough, so Frank laid it on thick. He gripped the club like a baseball bat, swirled around like a whirling dervish and hit the ball straight down the middle all day. Frank thought the man knew what was up after awhile, but he just swallowed his pride and paid. Later, when they were splitting up the take in the motel, Ti talked about taking Frank to St. Louis to work the same business on another guy, but Frank passed. Nobody, but nobody, matched up to Ti in nerve.

I did go on the road with Ti, and there was one incident that made me realize the man would stop at nothing to win a bet. We were in Ardmore, Oklahoma, mixed up in a tough nine-hole match against a couple of long hitters, $1,000 a man. We were dead-even going into the 7th hole, and I remember telling Ti we'd better shape up, the holes were running out.

"I know, I know," he said with a far off look, like he was

planning something. "Now you just go along with what I'm gonna do, and don't let it affect your game."

I had no idea what he had in mind, but then all of a sudden, he started staggering around like he was dizzy. Then he leaned down into the golf cart, put his head on the floor, stuck his feet straight up in the air, and started coughin' and wheezin'. Ti was about 75 years old at that time, he stood 6'4", and weighed maybe 145 lbs. soaking wet—he looked like walking death. He went through this routine for about five minutes and the other guys were major-league shook. They wanted to know if he wanted an ambulance, to go to the hospital, whatever.

"Oh no," he said, "Nooo....I'd have to pay y'all. We got three holes to go and I'm damn sure gonna finish this match if it kills me."

Well now these guys are watching Ti's every move, afraid that he's about to croak on the course. Naturally, they start topping the ball, shanking shots—they could hardly concentrate at all. I could see that they didn't have a prayer, so I laid back a bit and beat them on the last hole with a par.

That must have been around 1968 or 1969. We hooked up to go on the road a couple more times, but once he hit eighty, he went downhill pretty fast. He tried to get me some games up in Roanoke, but when I got there, I could see it wasn't really happening. I got a Christmas card from him one year, then talked to him on the phone a few months after that and his voice sounded kind of feeble. Then, in 1974, I heard that he had died at a nursing home. The guy that told me said that to the very end, Ti was bookin' bets, flashing the cash, and trying to sucker the old folks every which way. They just don't make 'em in his mold anymore.

5

On the Road

The road can be a lonely place—I don't care if you're a truck driver, a Bible salesman, or a golf hustler. There's only so much you can take of the Days Inns and the Dennys. Even going low-cost, the expenses will eat you up if you're not ringing the register all the time. And, of course, you miss the family. People think, oh well, he's just playing golf, how tough can it be? Well, while I try to have fun out there, I never was much of a "fun" golfer. In my mind, I'm out on the golf course trying to make money. In that respect, it's like a job.

Going on the road was easier for me when I was younger. All it took was a phone call and I was gone. Just tell me who, where, and for how much. I've had a set of clubs in my trunk now for close to forty years—a few pairs of golf shoes and extra shirts, too. It may be crazy, but after a couple of marriages, grown children, and a lifetime of bangin' that pill, I'm still game. Just don't make me drive too far—them tires tend to get bald.

The first time I really hit the highway—not counting those

little puddle-jumpers near home—was a mid-'60s trip I took down to Florida with Frank Stone. For me, it was a real eye-opener. Frank was a good, scufflin', scratch player who had been hustling the Miami area the previous few winters. He took me on as a partner and set up our action, which I assumed would be pretty fat, seeing as how he knew the scene and all. Frank was four years older than me, and as far as golf goes, he'd been around both sides of the track. By that I mean he'd gone to Wake Forest with Arnold Palmer, and he'd picked up the game as a kid with a rough-and-ready crowd at Hillcrest, a municipal course in Charlotte.

We hit the white line in Frank's yellow Riviera. Along for the trip was a fellow I'll call Willy, a good ole' country boy who didn't know the first thing about golf. Willy's field of expertise was raising hounds and shootin' dice—he was a master at that. He was a "tops" man, meaning he could slip a pair of dice into the middle of a craps game that absolutely could not "seven." Of course that meant that he wasn't too welcome around our dice games, but sometimes people would let him play provided he didn't ever throw.

Willy was also pretty good at shag dancing, which we found out when we pulled up to a juke joint off the road in Georgia. Willy put on a show dancing with some ladies, and after a half hour we had to drag him away. We stopped in Vero Beach to hit some balls at a range, and Willy made the mistake of trying to hit one golf ball—the first in his life. He took a mighty swing, whiffed, and threw out his back. He was in terrible shape the entire trip, and he just kept moaning, "Man, this golf is a rough game..."

Anyway, we called down from Vero to West Palm, and told them that we were on our way and to set up our game. I didn't have much money at the time, so we were splitting it up three ways, whatever we were going to win. We didn't think too much about losing.

Now Frank had said that we could take these guys—if we played well—but after the first day on a tough, windy course, I could see we had our hands full. They were, like ourselves, a couple of scratch players who liked to jack up the stakes. It doesn't take long to see that a guy can nail the ball off the tees and fire at the pins same as you do. We had all we could do to break even the first day, but we didn't have but a few hundred between us, so it's not like we could make this a week-long event. Hell, the greens fees alone would break us before the knife and fork would.

So the next day, Frank tells our opponents that this eighteen holes would have to be it, he couldn't be sticking around, and something to the effect of, "if anybody wants to gamble, let's get it on." We set the match for $500, $600—serious money, back then, not to mention that we didn't have it. Frank mumbled something to me about, "If we lose, I'll tell them I'll send them a certified check back from Charlotte." I didn't like it one bit.

We lost the front nine, badly. Frank went for a drink in the clubhouse and found Willy, who'd stayed behind with his sore back. Willy asked how we were doing. Frank told him we were getting creamed, and, as I later found out, he put together a getaway plan. I didn't know it, but Frank had doubled all of our bets for the back nine. The plan was that if we were losing, he would wave his hankie as we were coming up the 18th fairway—that was the signal to Willy that we had to stiff these guys and bolt. Willy would then get the car ready, back it up as near to the green as possible and push the trunk release. We would tell the guys that we had to put our bags away, and we'd meet them in the clubhouse to pay off, when actually we were going to run out on them.

But on the back side, things turned around full circle. Our opponents hit a wall, and even though Frank wasn't playing too well—he had a lot on his mind—I was draining putts from every which way. Coming up the 18th, I was five under par with the match locked up, when I took my glove off to shake out some perspiration. Willy took this as the signal, went and got the car, backed it up onto the course through a flower bed right up to the fringe of the green, and popped the trunk.

I didn't know what was going on, but any kind of way, it looked terrible. Frank said, "Jesus, he's going to get us killed," and went running as fast as he could to get Willy out of there. He and Willy were up by the car, with Willy yelling loud enough for everybody to hear, "Well, Leon gave me the damn signal!" The other guys caught the whole act and must have suspected something. In fact, when Frank came back to putt, they asked what was going on. "Oh, he doesn't know anything about golf courses," Frank told them. "I asked him to back the car around for us to put the clubs away, and he just got confused and brought it up a little too close."

The other guys paid up and laughed it off, saying they'd never seen anything like that before, and anyway, it wasn't their course getting wrecked. Willy helped things out by coming into the bar in his flamboyant way and announcing, "Gentlemen, these drinks are all going to be on me." But I was still a little shook up, even when we were up the road, heading out of Dodge with the money.

Frank did not like to lose and would go to any lengths to

avoid it. I found this out a number of times, but the one time that sticks out was a story he told me about a veterinarian he used to play down at Normandy Lakes in Miami who had a low handicap and liked to bet high. One day Frank and his partner, another scuffler, got out early, went into a storage area and got the guy's clubs. They proceeded to squirt varying amounts of caulking compound down into the shafts through the little hole that's on top of every grip. Now if you know anything about swing weight, a mere dollar bill on the end of a club will change the swing weight one degree, which to a fine-tuned golfer, can be a lot.

The guy never had a chance that day. He sprayed his ball all over the place, lost a bundle, and never got wise. "Desperate people do desperate things," Frank used to say.

Another time back in Charlotte, Frank got into a rival player's golf bag and "loaded" up some of his soft-covered, balata Titleists. He took a hypodermic needle and injected a couple of ccs of chloric acid into the ball's core. The acid eats up a bit of the inside of the ball, just enough to make it off center. You could still smash the ball, but it would fly all kinds of crazy ways. As precise a game as we were used to playing, it didn't take but a few bad hits to lose a match and drop some dough. Those doctored balls cost a poor sucker one grand that day. Desperate people do desperate things.

Florida was fertile ground for golf action, especially in the winter months. On another trip, Stone took me to Miami, where I took on Marty Stanovich, the legendary Fat Man. "Stan" was one of the great golf hustlers of all time. At 5'10", 275 lbs. and with one of the ungodliest golf swings you ever saw, Fat Man didn't look like much on the golf course, which played right into his hand.

The first day we locked horns was a real battle—twenty-seven holes with the wind just howling. We stayed even until the last nine, where he just blew me away—shot 30, which in that wind was like shooting 25. Against most people, Stan would fool around for fifty-dollar bets, get the game set up right, then really turn it on. Against me, he let it all out right away; he had to—we were sink and swim for about a week, with me sneakin' back in for the $1,500 I had dropped out of the gate.

Against others, good players even, I saw Fat Man play when he felt like it. He would never hit terrible shots; he flew the ball off-line exactly where he wanted it—right or left of the green, overclubbed or underclubbed—before making par. He was easily the best sand trap player I've ever seen. He wasn't trying to get up and down from the beach, he'd actually try to hole the ball. A lot of times he shot at bunkers on purpose to keep the games going. Then when the money got to where he liked it, he'd just flag the damn ball. You could not miss a shot to beat him— people liked to say that about my game.

With so much mutual respect, Stan and I pretty much stayed clear of each other over the years. We hooked up again on some teams action in the mid-'60s up at Bardmore Country Club in Largo, Florida, when I had a partner up there who was flush with funds. Stan sniffed this out and brought a hustling pro with him; we pretty much broke even, except for my partner who footed the bills. That's the way it goes a lot of times on the road; there's a money man who stakes most of the games. If you're playing high-dollar, it can be a real nice setup—no expenses, no risk, and a percentage of what you win.

When I returned to Charlotte in the springtime, I got a call from Stan, who was making his annual pass through Chicago and was looking to bring some new blood along. I packed up some sticks and flew up blind—that is, I didn't really know what Stan had going, except that we'd be partners. I knew beforehand that he locked it up pretty good, so there wasn't much downside. What I didn't know was that we'd be playing high-stakes golf against some heavy-duty, mob generals—"connected" boys is the way Stan put it when he picked me up at the airport.

Being a shrewd road man, Stan had established good relations with high rollers around the country. In Chicago, it just happened to be some Italian dudes who commanded respect. On the golf course, they were perfect gentlemen, paying off in cash from huge bankrolls while their bodyguards stood by. At first, I was a little nervous with a protection crew wearing overcoats in ninety degree heat and riding around in carts never more than a couple of yards from the head honcho. But I settled down once I realized that these guys respected me and the way I played.

Jackie was the top man, a sharp dresser with a 6 handicap, who liked to gamble. Most of the time, he had a tour player for a partner, but the two of them were no match for me and Stan. Playing at Medinah (the site of the 1990 U.S. Open) and other exclusive courses, we were taking down a couple of thou a day. In the evenings, Jackie would take me around town, showing me all the night spots he had a piece of. I was treated like royalty, and I guess Jackie had taken a liking to me. He didn't seem to mind losing the money, and after two weeks of play, he made me an offer that he thought I couldn't refuse.

Jackie wanted to put me on retainer. The deal was that he would pay me $1,000 a month, no obligations, just to have me available to fly up for golf games. Sometimes I'd be teamed with him; other times, I'd be a single, playing on his stake. "Every first of the month, you open your mailbox, you find a check from me," is the way he put it. Well, as much as I could go for a free paycheck, that whole deal had "pass" written all over it.

"Jackie," I told him, "I'm grateful for your offer, but I'm just a runabout golf hustler. I like to stay on my own and be independent."

A few months after that I found myself in Toledo, Ohio, without the Fat Man, again playing some dudes that I knew were involved in the rackets. Just making conversation, I mentioned Jackie's name, and my opponent pretended like he didn't know who I was talking about. He seemed a little nervous, and after I beat him that first round, he went to make a phone call. When he came back, he insisted I come over to his house for dinner. Later, after his wife had cooked a fantastic three-course meal, he passed me the keys to a new Lincoln and insisted I use it however long I was in town. I tried to refuse, but he wouldn't hear of it. The next day, he set me up with a sweet game against one of his cronies—a game I could play around with, ease up a little and still win. That night I received a call in my motel room.

"My man Le-on-e," came the voice, which I knew was Jackie. "I hear you're doin' all right with some of my boys down there." That's right, I told him, and thanked him for all the favors and the attention, which I knew was his doing.

48

"Hey, this is all family, we're talking about," he said. "You're family, too, Le-on-e, and the offer still stands." Again, I refused, polite as I could be. Jackie went on to tell me that if I ever had trouble collecting from anybody, anywhere, just give him a call, and he'd see to it that I got paid. I knew he probably could, and boy there were some hard times when I was tempted to drop that dime, but I never did. That was the last I ever heard from him.

For the best Florida action in the late '60s, Airco Golf Course in St. Petersburg was the place to be. It wasn't all that much of a course—flat, long, and nothing tricky—but man could you ever find a game. Airco was right next to an airport and the wind never let up. Most of the matches involved a group of top-notch, black golfers. Some were pros just then breaking through the color line on the PGA Tour, guys like cross-handed George Johnson, top wind player Nate Starks, and the long-hitting Jim Dent (now on the Senior Tour); then there was a whole group of others, characters that included Saginaw Pete, "Preacher Man" (an Irish Bible salesman), and one of my favorite opponents, George Wallace, a.k.a., "Potato Pie."

Pie was a tremendous shotmaker. I will always remember a trick he pulled off with his ball wedged down next to a railroad tie, and a cart path and steep bunker between him and the par-5 9th green. We were not allowing any relief, he lied two and needed a birdie to win the bet, but there didn't look to be any way for him to get up and down. I figured he'd pitch out safe to the side. Instead, he chopped down on the pill with a three-iron, had it bounce off of the path with overspin, and skip up through the trap on the green two feet from the cup for his bird. My partner, Jerome Bowman, looked over at me and said, "Damn, they don't even put that shit in the movies."

But I got Pie pretty good one time in a classic case of mind over matter. He came into the clubhouse moaning one day. "Pie don't feel so good," he said, talking about himself the way he always did. "Pie can't play today."

"I got something in the car for the Pie," I said, "something make the Pie feel better."

"What is it?" he asked.

"Don't ask me what it is. Just get you some coffee, take the pills I'm gonna give you, and you'll be ready to play in about fifteen minutes."

I went out and got some ordinary aspirin, which he took, and in about ten minutes he came strutting around. "Pie feels good now, let's go play." I ended up beating him out of $700 that day, but he wasn't done. "Let's go do something else," he said, suggesting we go play some cards over at the Pink Champagne, a motel where a lot of us stayed. Well, I didn't like that so much, and didn't feel like shooting pool either when he offered that. Then he came up with the idea of pitching to the line, and I said, "We sure can do that." I beat him out of $2,000 pitching, and busted him for all his cash.

That night, he went back to the motel and slept about twelve hours. When he came out to Airco the next day, he accused me of giving him "loser's pills." "Them things you gave me screwed my head all up. Pie couldn't think right."

"Pie," I said, "that wasn't nothin' but aspirin. I just wanted you in the golf game, that's all." He wouldn't have none of it, and for a long stretch, he wouldn't play me anymore, either.

"Stay away from the witch doctor," he was telling every-one. "Man give you the loser's pills."

One day I was playing Saginaw Pete Short who was pretty much the "manager" for a lot of these guys. Halfway up the 8th fairway, a group of FBI agents came up on Pete, talked to him a bit, then cuffed him and led him away. Preacher Man was also playing with us and had just settled an old debt with Pete. "Excuse me," he said, as the agents were leaving with Pete, "but could I get the $500 I just loaned him?"

Meanwhile, I didn't like it too much myself; I had Pete down three holes at $500 a side. The kicker is, Pete was somehow released and came back around the time we were teeing up at 13. He didn't say a word about what happened, honored the bets, and won another five bills from Preacher, which he dropped to me. I never did find out what the busi-ness with the feds was all about, and I never asked. That's just the way it was around Airco.

John Whitehead, the "Preacher Man," played me a lot of different games; I don't think he ever beat me once. He quit preaching to play golf, but he just didn't fit in. He wore funny old street clothes, looked like a guy who couldn't play, and he couldn't. The very last time we played, he suggested that we get away from Airco, where he thought I played too good. "I'm gon' get you on a course you don't know nothin' about," he said.

He took me over to Lone Palm, a course where I'd played three satellite tournaments and a whole mess of partners games teaming up with tour pro Andy Bean. I told Preacher he could scramble three balls from the front tees (meaning he could try every shot three times); I shot 61 with a ball going in the water, and that was all for the Preacher.

Another time, Jimmy Mann, a sportswriter down there, was playing a guy named George George. Like Preacher Man, "Gee-Gee" was a pretty regular donator. He'd bring $300 to the course and wouldn't leave until it was gone. This one day, George was stuck $100 and trying to get Jimmy to give him more strokes on the back side, when they both noticed a car on fire in the parking lot.

"Isn't that your wheels?" asked Jimmy.

"Give me two more strokes, and I won't worry 'bout the car."

They finished the round, Gee-Gee lost his three bills, and I don't know what ever happened to his car.

In 1968, I was in the St. Pete area looking for a well-known local golfer, a man I had heard wouldn't shy from any game, anywhere. J. C. Goosie is today a millionaire from having started (and later sold) the successful Space Coast Professional Golf Tour in Florida; back then, the Goose was a ramblin'-gamblin', hard-drinking, hard-living player. I guess you could say that indirectly, I played a part in setting him straight.

Goosie and I first met when I tracked him down one morning at the East Bay Country Club in Clearwater, where he worked as an assistant pro. I called over to see if he felt like playing me some $100 nassau, and he said OK (he had a deal there where he could leave for a good money match), just tell him when and where. He said that he could make it to Airco in a half hour; I didn't know he'd been up all night playing poker, but he seemed all right when he showed up.

On the 1st tee, we laid down the ground rules, $100 a side,

automatic one-down presses, then Goosie went off to get him a six-pack. He refueled with another six at the turn, and by the end of our round he was pretty lit, and he'd also lost $700. I later found out that Goosie got into his car that afternoon and swore to himself that he would never touch another drop of liquor.

When I called his club the next day, they told me he was sick in bed; that's what he'd told them to say—he was actually out hitting balls on the range. This went on every day for a week; he was still "sick" every time I called, and I finally gave up. Then one day he showed up at Airco. He said "I've come back to get you," which he did, in spades. He showed me some lights-out golf that day and clipped me for $1,100. But we became fast friends from then on and played a lot of golf with and against each other over the next five years. Last I heard, he's never had a drink since then.

Right around the time Goosie started his satellite golf tour, we both played many a round with a wild man named Eli Jackson. Eli owned carnivals, X-rated movie theaters, and some miniature golf courses. He was a fast talker, couldn't play much golf, and he loved to bet. I'll never forget the time he was carrying on about something or another, and we're all walking down the fairway looking for his drive. I asked Eli where he'd hit it, and he said he couldn't remember. We looked all over the place for a good while until one of the eyeballers following us around said Eli never had hit his ball. He'd been so absorbed in whatever he was talking about, he'd forgotten to hit—and that was for fifty dollars a hole!

Eli would pull into the lot in a big Rolls Royce, then go wheel around in his golf cart which had a special Rolls Royce grill on it. He had everything in that cart, mini-fridge, telephone (this was before cellulars)—he even had a TV in there, but I never saw him use it. Many's the time when I was entered in one of Goosie's golf tournaments, wasn't doin' any good, and I just pulled up in the middle of a round and went looking for Eli.

Eli wouldn't play anybody except Goosie or me. We both tried to give him more strokes—I believe I gave him seven a side—but he always refused. "If I can't play good enough with fourteen shots, I'll just quit," he would tell me; but he never did. One day, I brought along Gary Koch (a former tour player, who's now a TV commentator) just to change things up a bit. "Why'd you bring him with you," Eli asked me. "You're just bringin' people to win money that you'd be gettin'." I couldn't argue with him.

Unlike many of the guys I ran up with, I never really drank much. Not that I didn't have a drink now-and-again; I just never really had a taste for the hooch. I never did any drugs either, and I can't recall but about a handful of times when I saw pot being smoked around the golf course. Maybe it went on and I didn't know about it, but I like to think that golf and drugs just don't mix too well. If I did have a weakness back in my early days on the road, it was my occasional crazy tangles with women of questionable character. In that respect, I was a world-class lollipop.

There are a lot of invitations and offers made when you lead the kind of life I've led. It all depends on how you handle it. They let you know they're there if you want 'em. I guess you could say that women and golf don't mix—at least not the kind you run up with on the road.

On one trip down at Airco, I noticed a beautiful girl staying in the room next to mine at the motel. I couldn't miss her if I wanted to, since everywhere I went—coffee shop, parking lot, whatever—she was checking me out with these big brown eyes—"bedroom eyes," I'd guess you'd call them. It seemed like everytime I walked out of the room, she was standing there in some tight-fitting, sexy outfit, waiting for me to come out the door. Finally, after a couple of days of this, I struck up a conversation, and she was on my arm in a minute flat.

She was cute all right, and it took me about half a day to get all hung up. The first night we stayed up late, and it got worse, or better, however you want to look at it, all week long. She always wanted us to go out and have a drink, get a bite to eat, no matter what time of night it was. I was all mixed up; part of me was hooked on her, the other part kept reminding me that I was there to play golf. My game didn't suffer too bad, which was good since I was playing an extended team match with some $15,000 at stake.

Then, the last night we were together, she told me she was with the guys I was betting against. She said they wanted me to dump on my partner (lose on purpose), and we could all split up the money. I realized in a flash that plan A was to have me so whipped I couldn't play, and plan B was for her to talk me into double-crossing my partner—getting me one way or another. I told her she had the wrong guy for a "tank" job, so then she pleaded with me to do it for her, "for us," she even said.

She had me goin' so good that I even considered it. Like a fool, I was thinking about our future together. I went and played our match that day, on the square, of course, and I was in a total fog. I couldn't play a lick. My partner carried us, and we won $8,000. I headed back to the motel looking to lay out some fine wining and dining, but when I got there the baby-doll was checked out and gone—no note, nothin'. I never saw her again.

One trip back from Florida, I was cruising on near-empty in a Lincoln I had. Heading up the off-ramp of I–95 to get some gas, I spotted a red-headed girl in a maxi-coat, carrying a little overnight bag, hitch-hiking back up the on-ramp. Even from a distance, there was something about her I just had to get with, so I gassed up with a gallon-and-a-half's worth and tore off after her.

I pulled up, she jumped in, we got to talking, and hit it off pretty good. I knew she was a hard girl—she said her boyfriend had put her out and she was in the dumps—but she softened me up when she told me that she was headed for Macon to get a part-time job so that she could buy some Christmas presents for her kid. One thing led to another and after I bought her dinner, we checked into a motel around Valdosta.

When we got back on the road, I already had it in my mind that I'd talk her into coming with me to Charlotte. Hell, I was all ready to adopt her kid or at least go pick him up for Christmas. Suddenly, when we got to one of the Atlanta exits, she said she wanted to get out, this was as far as she was going. I said all right, but I wanted her to give me her number so I could swing back through on my way back to Florida in a week or so and see her again.

She said, "I'll get off right here," and started fumbling

through her purse, which I thought was to give me her number. Next thing I know she's got a gun pulled on me. She was shaking, with tears running down her cheeks. "Don't make me hurt you," she said. "I've never done this, but I need money." She was so out of sorts, I was afraid the gun, some kind of snub-nose, was gonna go off by accident. I dug down deep into my pocket and gave her all the cash I had, about $700 or $800, which she must have caught a flash of when I paid for the motel room. She thanked me, said she was sorry, and I left her there on the highway with my cash that she'd robbed. I'm glad she didn't know anything about the $10,000 that I had stashed in the trunk. That was a short but sweet relationship; I guess we never had all that much future.

6

Rivals

In my business, you tend to run into some of the same opponents over and over. You can't let it get too personal or you'll shoot some train-wreck rounds—guaranteed. It's easy enough to get caught up in who you're bumpin' heads with. There's just so much ego involved in being a good player, and people get affected by personalities. "Jeez, I just want to beat this sumbitch so bad..." is not a positive thought to start a round off with. When it gets personal, there's that much extra riding on the game, and it's tough to overcome. Little mistakes become all that much harder to shake off.

But I have had some very regular customers over the years, call 'em rivals if you will. If you play in the same places long enough, you practically wind up married to the games you make and the people who make them. After bangin' heads so many which ways, you tend to become just a wee bit familiar with your regular players.

Charlie Simpson, a typical, hard-core, renegade gambler, was one of the first cats I ever started playing with regularly. He never had a social security card, gambled all his life, and knew every cheat and con in the book. He was a huge man, didn't take up golf until late in life, and when he did, he flat-out mastered the game. I mean that he got it to where he could shoot anywhere between 68 and 88—whatever score he needed to win. He was a big bullshitter, had a great sense of humor, and when he drank, he had a mean-ass temper.

When Charlie and I first started playing, my game was on the climb, and we had to change the spots all the time, since Charlie was anything but a sucker. If I beat him playing without my woods, then next time I'd have to play him without my two-, three-, and four-irons, and so on; there was always some serious adjusting to make, and it proved to be a fairly simple way to handicap a game.

I'll never forget the time I played Charlie with a putter and a wedge, and him having to putt kicking the ball. He was pretty good with his feet; that's just the kind of thing a golf hustler, with a lot of spare time on his hands, will practice on the putting green—when nobody's watching. He had a nice little technique where he'd hit it with his instep and pretty much put the right speed on it. Anyway, coming to the last hole, Charlie was looking at a little ten-footer for a win (and practically an automatic two-kick to tie the match). Somehow, he swiped at the ball and caught it on the underside of his shoe and it only went about a foot. The next boot looked right on the money, but it just lipped out, and Charlie lost the entire match. He got real hot, went straight for the hooch, and everybody stayed clear of him for a few days.

I got the worst of his temper one day after we'd all been sitting around Eastwood drinking Purple Jesus (that's vodka and grape juice) and playing liar's poker. People would drop out, and, eventually, it was just me and Charlie playing for what the others had lost. Charlie got real polluted and lost several hundred cash and another $400 that he owed me. Then he started grumbling something about how he wasn't going to pay me. I headed out to the parking lot and he followed me.

He kept reaching into his pocket like he was going to pull out this eight-inch switchblade that he always carried. I said, "Don't you pull that thing on me," knowing full well that Charlie would cut me in a minute. I told him to go on home, and sleep it off.

He said "Don't you tell me what to do, smartass." Well I knew there was trouble there, and, for protection, I had grabbed a handle off a pull cart. Charlie came out with his shiv. I swung around just in time, caught him flush upside the head, and knocked him under his truck.

Someone drove him home. He called me at four o'clock in the morning, not exactly apologizing, asking me why I hit him so hard. He grumbled that I would find my money waiting for me at Eastwood the next day, and it was there, the way I knew it would be. Charlie could be a dangerous, mean-ass hothead, but he paid his debts.

The last time I played Charlie, I beat him on the 18th hole for a few hundred dollars. He looked at me like he wanted to kill me, the man hated to lose so much. He went into his pocket, and I thought oh-oh, here it comes, but he just pulled out that fat wad, peeled off some C-Notes, and said, "Have fun spending this, 'cause that's the last red cent you'll ever get off me." We never played another game, and he dropped dead of a heart attack about two years later.

* * *

Les Furr was a golfer who couldn't play a lick and couldn't win a bet either. It's not that he liked to lose—he didn't appear to want to, anyway—but he couldn't do anything but fork it over. He was about a 16, 17 handicapper and had plenty of other available games. Yet, he always wanted to test himself with me. We played dozens of ways over the years, and I'm searching to recall if he ever came out ahead once—I honestly don't think he ever did.

Les enjoyed the creative aspects of his handicapping. I didn't really have to stretch my imagination much; he did it for the both us. He had me playing one-handed, from the golf cart, left-handed, one club, whatever. Then he would mix variations on what I did, him playing ladies' tees or two balls from the white tees. It was almost as if the losing didn't matter as long as the game was wild enough.

Once Les talked me into playing my ball with a lacrosse stick, while he played regular golf. I had never seen a lacrosse game or a stick, but I figured, what the hell, he wants to play it, I'll go along with it—just let me have a little practice.

I didn't fare too well at first, but then I looked up Jim McNulty, a local boy who was an all-American lacrosse player in college. Jim worked with me for about an hour and got me to where I could throw a golf ball properly with the stick—make it come out straight and travel about 160 yards. That's really all I needed to beat Les, since he was letting me chip and putt once I got to the greens. When he lost, he kept telling everybody "I just don't believe that." Well, I don't know, was I supposed to only get ninety yards on my throws or flings or whatever they were? Hell, Les was the one who thought up the game.

The last time we ever played, I played left-handed, borrowing Les's clubs, since he was a natural lefty. I had hit some shots lefty, but never played a whole match that way. What you have to do is really concentrate on contact and sort of come across the ball, play for a controlled slice. Left-handed putting wasn't bad—I'd had a lot of practice at that—but chipping can be tough. You can't really sweep the ball; you have to more-or-less bump-and-run it.

Funny thing, I started playing pretty good lefty that day and bore down all the harder. I couldn't let up, because I didn't have the club control to do so. Besides, I had way too much killer instinct for my own good back then. So, I won the cash that day, but I also lost another customer. "If you can play me and beat me with my own clubs," Les had said, before we teed up, "I ain't never gon' play you again." That time he meant it, but I was too mule-headed to realize it at the time.

One of the toughest nuts I ever had to crack was Bobby Howard, a top player and part-owner of Sedgewood, the course I liked so much down in South Carolina. After I beat Bobby and his pals, and the whole town of "sweators" out of thirty large that one time, I was always welcome back. See, in their minds, that money was supposed to make a U turn at some point, and of course, some of it actually did. But I knew I always had a game if I wanted it.

One of my worst episodes with Bobby was what Catfish and I remember as, the terrible "thump-in." Catfish had driven down with me and was betting a ton on my match. Bobby wasn't such a long hitter, so he said he'd play me for $2,000 leaving out the par 5s. That didn't help me any, since I loved long holes. But I figured that I was bulletproof so I took the game. On the par-4 second hole, Bobby was in with a bogey, and I had a five footer left for a birdie. We played "gimmes" on pretty much every putt inside eighteen inches, but a player had to say "that's good," or "pick it up," whatever. I rolled my putt up to the lip, bent over, and thumped it in with my thumb, like a marble shot. As we're walking off the green Bobby asked me what I had. "Four," I told him.

He said, "I don't think you actually have a score," he said, looking me right in the eye. "You have done forfeited the hole. We're not playin' no fifty dollar nassau; we're gamblin' high. Unless somebody gives you a putt, you have to knock it in the hole."

I blew up, I mean, with my game, that is. As hot as I was with Bobby, I couldn't say anything, and he knew it. Rules are rules. I hit my very next tee shot in the water, and while I did manage to calm myself down, I never did recover from those two holes. The "thump-in" cost me and Catfish $4,000 that day, and you learn from your mistakes. Unless I hear, "THAT'S GOOD" loud and clear, I putt everything out.

The most rounds I've played against any one individual were played against Bob Bryant, a great player who gave me as many fits as I gave him. We locked up the better part of the '60s, and I'd say that I got the best of the war, even if I did lose some battles.

Bryant was athletic, he had great golf skills, and was a tough man to beat, as crazy as he was, which was plenty. He'd come to Eastwood after work, late in the afternoon, and liked to play a nine-hole match. The first five times we played, I don't think he shot worse than 31. He would only agree to play me eighteen holes at Eastwood if we also played a full round at Tanglewood, his home track. I shot 63 there and beat him, then turned around and shot 61 at Eastwood. I think that day stayed with him a long time.

Bryant had pro-tour aspirations and practiced golf just about every waking hour that he wasn't working in the furnace business. He had a short, jerky motion with a backswing that never got up much past his shoulder. This proved to me that you can take about any swing and make it work, if you practice enough. Funny thing was, as good as he played, he'd just as soon cheat you if he could get away with it. He had the crookedest caddy helping him out, moving the ball and stuff. You practically had to keep one eye on Bryant and the other one on his caddy.

One of Bryant's favorite bets was that he could make three from the top of the clubhouse to the tenth hole, a distance of about 175 yards. It wasn't an easy shot, especially off the sloping shingles. He lost a bunch of times on that, before he changed to, if he made it in four, it was a tie. It seemed like he enjoyed the crowd this bet would draw, more than he did his action, which wasn't that good.

There was no limit to how crazy a proposition Bryant would take on. One time Catfish bet him $200 that he couldn't shoot 75 walking backwards to every shot, the entire round. Bryant got totally twisted on that, and was about falling over after three holes, when he quit and paid off. (I tried to beat a guy offering that bet in Vegas years later, and he trimmed my ass; I guess that walking backwards affects some people and not others.) Another time, Bryant got Catfish back by shooting 34 in less than thirty minutes (they had bet that he couldn't shoot 38).

Then there was once when Bryant had to run backwards on the back nine, touching every flagstick in X amount of time. He fell down five times trying to get up the hill on 15, but he was still way ahead of his pace. He took off like a backpedalin', halfback on 16, yelling "I'll take a hundred! I'll take a hundred!" Somebody yelled back, "settle up!" and Bryant fell face down on the ground. "I ought to be in Hollywood," he said, "makin' y'all think I had a chance on that bet. I couldn't a made it another ten feet."

Bryant was the cockiest golfer you'd ever want to play. We were playing one of our many matches and he was crying about his tee shot on a par 3, an eight-iron that wound up about eighteen feet from the hole. (Bryant was a hall-of-fame complainer, and it was something you'd have to ignore; if you'd get to feeling sorry for him and back off even the slightest bit, he'd be back up at your throat in a minute.) I said "if you think you can do better, I'll let you play another ball." Of course I never thought he'd take me up on it. He did, and knocked it right in the hole. The amazing thing about that day was when we came around a second time, I aced the hole myself.

Early one morning, I was about to head home from a Charlotte poolroom, when I got a call from Catfish who said that Bryant was trying to track me down. He said that he had some "easy pickin's," some boys who wanted to throw some money around in a partners match in Myrtle Beach that day. I was pretty tired, but if we wanted to make the game we had to hit the road right then, which, of course, we did for what was about a three-hour drive.

We got to the Beach as the sun was coming up, got some coffee and donuts, and met Bryant at the course. He said the others would be there in a half-hour or so. I hit some balls, went and putted a bit, and an hour later, our opponents still hadn't showed. After two, three hours, it was obvious that they weren't going to show. Bryant says, "Well, hell, we might as well play each other while we're down here."

So we did, $1,000 a side, $3,000 being all that I brought with me. Back at Eastwood, I had been getting the best of Bryant, but it didn't take me long to realize that he knew every roll on this track. He got me pretty good, and coming up the 18th fairway, I was pretty well ready to go home broke. He surprised me when he sidled up to me practically foamin' at the mouth saying, "Sucker, I done trapped you. There weren't no other guys. That was just a setup for me and you to play, and I knew I could beat you here. Now I got you busted, I ain't gonna give you money for a Coca-Cola and a pack of Nabs."

Well, I was steamed, but I was also broke, and he knew it. Then a funny thing happened. It was getting dusky-dark, and in the parking lot, Catfish saw this guy, Charlie, a money-man he knew from the Beach courses. Catfish told Charlie what went down, and Charlie offered to stake me hole by hole.

I knew Bryant wouldn't back off. He was a greedy bastard, and his ego was flying. Within a couple of minutes, we're back on the course playing $500 a hole, and I am stickin' it, I mean flat out stickin' it. Just about when we could hardly see the balls anymore, I had won all my money back. Then, later on, we beat Bryant out of $2,500 shooting craps in the club-house and about broke him. I offered him a Coke and a pack of Nabs, even dinner if he wanted, but he just ran out.

I haven't seen Bryant in years, but I did hear a recent story about him that sounded about right. "I got the damnedest thing to tell you," he reported to a mutual friend of ours. "I died about six, or seven months ago, then I came back. I had a heart attack and they took me to the hospital emergency where they worked on me, gave me some kind of shock. I was floating up on the ceiling watching as they worked on me. I found out later it was only about five minutes, but it seemed like forever. I didn't want to come back, it felt so good. But I did, and here I am, and now I ain't playin' worth a shit."

7

Get a Hunch, Bet a Bunch

There's an old warning in the South that pretty well covers all betting propositions. It goes like this: if a man comes up with a new deck of cards and wants to bet you that he can make the jack of spades jump out and spit tobacco juice in your ear, don't bet, or you'll wind up with empty pockets and an ear full of tobacco juice. There's got to be a lot of truth to that, since where I come from, the only person who would back up such a wild come-on with cold cash would be a stone-cold locksmith. If it was me, I'd bet the farm that there was a tobacco-spitting jack in that deck.

I can pretty well speak for that kind of thing around the golf course, having been on both the winning and losing side of many a proposition ever since I can remember. More than likely, if I offer to bet that I can shimmy up a flagpole to hit a six-iron across the parking lot onto the 18th green—that means I been there before, somewhere along the line, and I figure to have the edge. Usually, but not always.

*　　*　　*

Probably the out-and-out dumbest move I ever made was back in 1977, the time I bet I could hit a golf ball over the Las Vegas Hilton. I heard they still talk about it out there. I know they do around Charlotte, 'cause it seems like I never stop hearing about it. Needless to say, I had never tried the shot before. If I had, I would never have gotten trapped by such a half-looped, wild-assed, crazy notion.

Amarillo Slim is the one who thought it up and brought it up. He's a poker champion, a legendary gambler out of Texas and Vegas, but truth be told, he doesn't really have all that much gamble in him. Slim likes a lead-pipe cinch, which he sure wasn't getting on this particular afternoon when I was beating up on one of his boys, a college kid from out West that he was staking. We were coming off the 17th green with Slim stuck four bets for $8,000 and all closed out. He tipped back his cowboy hat, started stroking his chin and asked me if I reckoned I could clear the hotel with a golf ball from where we stood. Since I had been crushing my five-wood, long and high, it seemed like a sporty offer, so I stopped and looked it over. I must have gotten sun stroke.

The Hilton was the next property over from the golf course. Problem was, buildings that stand by themselves in the desert look a hell of a lot closer than they really are—it's an optical illusion, and on top of that, my vision was getting a little worse around that time.

Well, I eyeballed it for awhile, and it just seemed like I ought to be able to put a six-iron on top of the roof—crazy when you consider it was twenty-five stories high. Don Cherry, the singer, was with us—he had a slice of my action with Slim—and he told me right off to leave it alone. "Don't mess with it," he kept telling me. "You can't do it. King Kong can't do it. There's just no way."

Sometimes that's all I need to hear. Slim and I started chewing it over, and now he was calling a stipulation. My ball would have to travel over the "I" on the big orange Hilton sign. "Leon, you gon' have to 'dot the I,' if you want any of my money," he was saying.

I wasn't going for any of that. I knew the whole deal was iffy, getting it that high up, and I certainly didn't want the added pressure of having to aim the ball over a target. I thought it was a negotiating ploy on Slim's part, but he wouldn't let it go. "Got to dot that I, if you want anymore from me."

At that point, Gene Skinner, one of the railbirds who'd been sweating my match, jumped in. "I got $3,000 says you cannot hit a regular golf ball over the Hilton with a regular golf club from right here on this spot," he said, standing on the 18th tee. You've got to be specific about these propositions or you can get stung easy.

"Gimme five tries," I said.

"Three."

"Got me," I told him, deciding to take a shot at it.

We put all the cash up, sixty one-hundred-dollar bills, with thirty on each side, speared by the tee blocks. Now I had bit—hook, line, and sinker—and all that was left was for them to reel me in. Funny thing is, Slim, the sure-thing artist, wasn't even in on the bet—not that I knew of anyway. That made me feel a little better about my chances, but you can't tell about these things. The guy who brings the bet up and the guy who winds up taking the action might be going partners all along.

Anyway, I really didn't care whose money I was up against—by now I had built up my confidence. I got out my five-wood and teed it up so high I about needed a step ladder to hit it. For loft, I opened up the clubface as much as I could without losing distance, gave her a mighty wallop, and watched the ball take off. About four seconds later, I got that sinking feeling, when the ball reached its peak about nine, ten floors up—it hit between a couple of windows. The ball had gotten almost to the top of its parabola not even half-way up the damn building, and I knew I'd popped it about as good as I could.

People don't usually laugh when you lose money— it's not considered good form. But that shot had the railbirds all busted up. I didn't bother to hit another ball; I really didn't feel like breaking any windows. Of course all the sweators wanted me to take my two other tries; this was the most fun they'd had all day. I wasn't about to give anybody that satisfaction.

Later on, Don stepped it off and came up with a distance of 208 yards to the base of the hotel. Then he went and got a slide rule and came up with something like I would have had to hit the ball some 175 yards high to clear the damn thing.

One good thing that came out of my Hilton fiasco was that they started running at me pretty good after that. It kind of made me out to be a sucker, and I started getting some pretty nice games. I guess the idea was, play Leon a match; while you're at it you might trap him on some locked-up, can't-lose side action.

But the downside, besides droppin' the $3,000 that day, was when the story somehow made its way into *Sports Illustrated*—in the front part where they put the funny sports stuff from the past week. It wouldn't have mattered, anybody having fun at my expense, but what got me is when they had Slim saying, "Leon Crump is the best money golfer in the whole world." I didn't need that. When I got back home, I couldn't land a game for months. It's amazing to me, but guys I had been bumpin' heads with for years would all of a sudden back off because of something they read in a magazine. "No way," they would say. "I'm not gambling with the best money player in the whole world."

Proposition bets are a routine part of golf gambling down South. It's all part of trying to get a game up, trying to get people to bet when they might otherwise not want to. Now, by proposition bets, I am also including wild and crazy handicapping—letting my opponents play from the ladies' tees, me playing with one foot in the golf cart, or hitting the ball from under paper cups, playing with only one club, and stuff like that. Some people might think that these are sucker plays, and maybe sometimes they are. But more often than not, it's just an attempt to stimulate action with people who think you're too strong for them to play *real* golf with you.

Early on at Eastwood I learned that once you start dusting people with your golf, you've got to come back with some crazy games, if you want them to play anymore. A lot of times, it's the novelty aspect of propositions that appealed to people. If they were going to lose, they wanted entertainment value for their money. They didn't just want to see me stick it to the pin while they're hacking around in the weeds; they wanted me to do something outrageous, to *earn* my money.

For example, there's the old hustle of playing out from under paper cups. The trick here is to place a twelve- or sixteen-ounce cup upside down over the ball when you tee it up, and you do the same thing on your shots to the green (once on the green you just putt regular, or maybe one-handed, left-handed, whatever the spot might be). I played a lot of guys this way.

What most people never realized, was that the ball tended to go perfectly straight out from under those cups. On the tee shots, I would just line up, take a normal swing, trying to hit a little ways up on the cup, and I swear the ball took off straighter than ever. On the iron shots, I had to make sure that I hit where the cup met the ground. As soon as the hit is made, the cup flips open on its side from the force of impact. I also think the slickness from the wax hitting the ball on the near side of the cup takes all the spin off the ball and causes it to fly straight as an arrow. Try it some time—just bring plenty of cups.

Stuart Bragg played me a-hundred-and-one ways. It didn't take him long to pass on the paper cups, but we did get creative in other games. I would sometimes let him play the best of two balls from the ladies' tees while I played the back tees or variations on that. This is a tough bet, especially on a course where the ladies' tees are way up. The first time we ever played it, some eyeballer yelled something to Bragg about ladies having to wear proper skirts on the course, but Bragg never looked up. Business was business, and a bet was a bet.

One of my losing prop bets to Bragg was one that's usually foolproof. In this case I got beaten by modern medicine. The idea here is to let a guy have as many drives as he wants to off every tee; he can pick the best one. Usually, about halfway through the round, the effort from trying to swing so hard so often will take its toll, especially on a hot day, and your

74

opponent will be one swing away from falling flat on his face. But not Bragg, who had a pacemaker that kept him going as strong as an ox. He never did get tired, and he sure played off some beautiful drives—sometimes after hitting five or six tries. That prop worked out to be a reverse trap.

I also played Bragg that he could tee it up anywhere—fairways, rough, or sandtraps. This was a popular spot, especially at an unmanicured course like Eastwood where you could get a lot of bad lies. There was a real tough hombre named Sanford Red who played everybody that way. As a matter of fact, Red carried a couple of foot-long tees he had had specially made up. When his ball fell into any kind of shallow water hazard, he would roll up his pant legs, stick that long peg in the drink, and play his ball like off a batting tee. It was something to see.

Red was a bad-news, country gangster. Ask him to pay you what he owed, and he'd like to draw his gun on you, what we call "throwin' down." Red was always packin' and always throwin' down on somebody. You couldn't really get rid of him—it's not like we called the cops whenever this sort of thing happened. One day somebody blew Red away with a double-barreled shotgun, right in his driveway in front of his house. They never found out who did it, but they surely had a long list of suspects.

One of my stongest games was offering to play people with nothing but a wedge and a putter, while they would play all of their clubs. This is an adjustable proposition. If I got beat, I would ask for one or two more clubs; if I won, I might try just a putter or a wedge alone.

Playing the putter alone is an acquired skill that comes from my days playing one club in the caddy yards. Of course, you have to use a blade-style putter. The idea is to catch it just right on the upswing, and I can generally get at least 200 yards off the tee. On the second shot, the approach shot, the idea is to choke down a little on the club and kind of chop it. Again, if you get it right, the ball will hit short of the green—say a shortish par 4—and scoot right on up there like a greased bullet.

Playing with the wedge alone can be plenty tough too. I'd need a bunch of golf balls—especially in the days before two-piece "hard" balls—because I seemed to tear up the ball every time I caught it full. What you want to do is hit a controlled "skull shot" with the edge of the blade. With the old, soft balata balls, you can pretty much slice a ball in half after a few hits. Putting with a wedge is not as hard as it seems; again, blade the club and take a slow, short backswing. You see pros do it when they're caught along the fringe. In that situation, the shot is actually easier with a wedge than with a putter.

One time I bet a bunch of guys at Eastwood that I could reach a 550 yard, par 5, with three, eight-iron shots. It really wasn't so hard, after I'd gone over to a plumber friend of mine and bent my eight-iron down to about a five.

When my timing is good, I've found that I can do seemingly amazing things with a putter. From 140, 150 yards, I can fly a ball to a green, cut it and stop it on a dime, and actually get spin on it. One of the benefits of one-club propositions is the psychological edge, the surprise factor of what it is that you're actually doing. If I get up on the tees with a putter and knock it out there right up next to somebody using a driver, they'll look up at me like "What is this?" Same thing when you knock in a ten-footer with your wedge a few times. People don't want to believe what they're seeing, which of course will affect the way they play.

On the subject of putter-play, here's a trap that I would suggest everybody stay away from, because it's a stone loser every time: you get to have your ball on the green in "regulation," that is, you get to be putting for a birdie every time, while I play regular golf trying to beat you; the only catch is, I get to choose where to place your ball on the green on every hole.

The first person I ever tried this bet out on was Scoop Jennings, one of the best putters at Eastwood. On the greens, Scoop fancied himself the world's greatest. He called his putter, an old Bullseye blade job, the "cobra." Time and time again he would get up on the 1st tee, pull that sucker out of his bag and shake it at you. "The cobra's gonna' get you," he'd say, practically shoving the thing in your face. "The cobra's gonna get you." It rarely did, since the rest of Scoop's game never really measured up.

One day I offered to let Scoop putt for bird on every hole, since he claimed to be such an expert putter. We would play regular match play golf, and his total on any hole would be whatever he got after putting. He jumped on it, thinking he had a mortal lock. I've never seen any player three-putt so many holes in one round. Think about it: there are some devilish places and distances to putt from on any green, and he would have the pressure of trying to get up and down every time. It didn't take any genius on my part to have him putting across a couple of time zones, sometimes with roller coaster breaks if the green set up that way. Meanwhile, I think I shot 74 and beat him by about nine strokes. Last I'd heard, he and the "cobra" had moved to New Orleans.

Balance is a key to any good golf swing. If you want to discover this for yourself, try hitting the ball off one foot or keeping one foot inside the golf cart. I found this out a few times while trying out some crazy one-foot bets. This is only the kind of thing I would try against a 17, 18 handicapper.

I guess that hitting the ball from a golf cart must be sort of like playing polo, which I don't know much about either. I do know that you have to watch your backswing, bring it down from way outside, to keep it from clanging against the cart. Once I tried playing every shot totally from inside the cart—except putting or trap shots of course—and I didn't fare so well.

Now playing on one foot was another case entirely—kind of a trick, in a way. The stipulation was that I could have only one foot on the ground while I was addressing or was hitting the ball, but I could save myself from falling down. What I did was stand on my left foot, but when I made contact, the right foot would sort of slide down to step over. I could almost "cheat" by getting the slightest bit of two-foot balance on the follow through. I got to where I could actually play with that technique.

One of the most amazing bets that I've ever been offered was when a fellow named Terry Florence—he's now a pro somewhere in Virginia—bet me that he could break 80 playing from his knees. It was the damnedest thing, but Terry shot 75 doing just that. I lost $300 watching that sucker put some real mustard on that ball and I still don't understand how. He used a set of junior clubs since he was so much closer to the ground, but I'm still amazed at the full-body turn Terry was able to generate without the benefit of proper balance.

One proposition bet that comes up every now and then has to do with throwing the golf ball—not so much for accuracy as for distance. The longest thrower I ever saw was James Black, a legendary black golfer from Charlotte who I've teamed up with over the years. Black would bet that he could get a ball to the green on a par 5 in three throws. (This again was a cinch since Black could also throw a ball through the uprights on a football field from the opposite end zone—on the fly!) On the par 5 bet, Black would usually let up on his second throw to make it look good, then let her rip on the third and just get there.

Black had another golf ball trick which was how many balls he could stuff into his mouth. I've seen him take down the cash with four new Titleists, lips closed, but he could actually get five in there—I picked up a dinner check once just to get to see it. Five is nothing short of incredible. If you're like me, you can barely fit one ball in there, and I would suggest being real careful testing this out. Hint: removable choppers are a big help.

I had a partner named Sparky who would bet anybody that he could throw a ball farther than they could hit a wedge. This too is pretty strong—means he's got to throw it at least 150 yards. Sparky trapped me once at Sunset Hills, in Charlotte, betting me $100 I couldn't fling it across the lake at the 15th hole (a par 3 from the front tees). It looked to be about seventy-five yards, so I gave it a shot and never even got it close. I threw my arm out and couldn't play for three months.

Another favorite spot was to let the other guy throw my ball back toward the tee, underhand, once on every hole. Again, he'd be playing his regular ball, and throwing in traps or bushes wasn't allowed. I gave this bet to my ole' pal Catfish, and he about had me cooked by the time we got to the 7th at Eastwood, a long par 3. I knocked it ten feet from the pin and stood back about fifty yards or so to wherever he was going to leave me. Somehow—I guess he was trying to put something extra on it—the ball slipped from his hand at the top of his toss and landed three feet from the cup. I holed out for a bird. Catfish cussed me up and down, and paid off. He had the nuts with that bet, but he got so hot at himself, he just had to let it go.

One time, back in the early '80s, at the Pawtuckett Golf Course, I was playing a whole mess of guys such a whole mess of games that I've forgotten most of them. Pawtuckett is closed now, but back then it was gambler's heaven. If you made the kind of matches I did, you were sure to have the eyeballers following you around. On this particular day, there must have been a dozen carts trailing us by the time we got to the 8th hole—it looked like a little convoy.

Now the tee for the 8th was about a hundred feet high up over a dogleg-left that ran out about 260 yards into a narrow fairway with woods on both sides before turning another 160 yards home. It was a real man-eater as far as leaving yourself a good second shot. Before I teed up, I made some joke about how I ought to try to fly the woods and go for the green off the drive.

Jeez, you'd have thought that I was looking to buy a couple acres of Tidewater swamp the way the offers came flying. Within about five minutes, I had negotiated $1,500 in bets that I could not land the ball on the green in ten tries. I made it on my very first shot.

Not that I ever expected or wanted to. On a bet like that, you're best off hitting the mark somewhere around the middle or late tries. You want to avoid looking like the favorite, or else you'll just be killing your future action. First try kind of sticks with people; they tend to remember a shot like that, especially if it costs them.

Actually it hadn't exactly been my first try. What set that bet up was a memory from a couple of years earlier, when I had knocked my ball deep out-of-bounds on the same hole. At that time I realized as I was reloading that the only chance I had of halving the bet was to go for the green as the crow flies. I lost the hole anyway—I hit a greenside trap, and I think I double bogeyed or something—but I did recall clearing those trees with a little room to spare. This time around, I wish I'd made it look a little luckier. But I sure as hell didn't tell anybody that I'd been there before.

We had a lot of crazy, cross-country bets at Pawtuckett. Once they were saying that I couldn't bogey the first hole starting from inside the men's shitter. This was another toughie, since the toilet door was pointed the wrong way, away from the hole. What I did was chip out to the gravel parking lot, which left me about an eight-iron over the clubhouse to get back into the first fairway about 225 yards from the green. I caught it thin and it skidded off the roof and overspun out to where I could handle it—as lucky a shot as I've ever hit. I got home from there and two putted to win the bet.

*　　*　　*

There's always been a ton of action at Myrtle Beach in South Carolina. Robber's Roost was one of the prime courses where a lot of games were made back in the '80s. It turned out to be a pretty good name for a club, since so many thieves hung out there. I had my share of big games at the Roost, but one bet I made with Leonard Thompson, now a standout tour player, stands out the most.

There was misty rain one day, and nobody seemed to want to do anything. After the usual back-and-forth "I'll do this...you'll have to give me that...," I struck up a "worst ball" proposition with Thompson. The worst ball bet means that the player is always hitting two shots and I make him pick the worst. In other words, if he hits a drive 250 yards down the middle, go on and hit another one; if that one goes in the rough, or better yet, the woods, well, he'll have to fight it from there. If he makes an eight-foot putt to save par, he'll have to sink it again. I bet that Thompson couldn't break 78 that way—in the rain, of course.

I still don't understand it, but I lost that bet. Thompson didn't make a bad hit over what was the equivalent of two rounds, since he had to take double the total of shots. If he ever got in a little trouble, like under the lip of a bunker, he blasted out, back-to-back, inside three feet. He fired a 74, and I got soaked watching him do it. It's lucky that I only had $1,700 to bet, because I would have put more up if I had it. In fact, I'm lucky I'm not still paying off today—that's how sure I was of that deal.

8

Collecting

A bookie once told me that winning the money wasn't any big deal; collecting was the hard part. I've felt exactly the same way at many a time. There used to be more, but nowadays, there's not all that much money floating around in gambling circles. You never know if a guy is playing you on "air," meaning he hasn't got but maybe five dollars in his pocket. Sometimes, I know I'm taking a chance, but I'll play anyway, figuring I'm not supposed to lose. Now here's an awful thought: I'll bet there have been times when I lost to someone where I didn't have anything to win and didn't know it.

I used to play at a course up in Norfolk, Virginia, where the club pro took match money up front and put it in a safe; that way nobody got shorted. There was a reason for that and I liked that they did it. Myself, I can truly say I never stiffed anybody on a bet. Even if I had to sell a car, which I did a few times, or, when I was younger, had to go borrow money from my daddy, I always paid off.

Sometimes you know a guy's got the money, but even then

you might not get paid. Let me give you a worst case scenario, something that happened to me that was pretty extreme.

I was down at Airco, in Florida, playing a $2,000 Nassau against a guy we called the "Short Man." Playing anybody down there could be rough, so after "flashing" each other our rolls (showing we each had the money), we agreed to pay off the first part of the bet after nine holes, before we played on. I lost the front side and paid what I owed. Then I won the back nine and the overall, so now it was Short Man's turn to cough up $4,000. I about fell over when he confessed to me that he only had $2,000.

I had just paid him $2,000, plus he had his original stake, so where in the hell was my money? He told me that before he teed off on the 10th hole, he'd seen a guy he owed money to, so he paid him. Things were about to get hot between us when Saginaw Pete jumped in and took over the debt. He paid me off. Pete was the "manager" for a lot of these guys. He had a pocketful of money, and was like a goodwill ambassador the way he'd get called on to use it. If Pete hadn't bailed Short Man out, that would have been a first for me— win the match, lose the dough.

One time I was playing a guy out at one of the par 3 courses for a few hundred dollars and having way the best of it. He was supposedly an assistant pro at one of the local courses and a part-time grade school teacher, so I knew he had some income.

Somehow or another—I think it was because the par 3 was closing around midnight—he talked me into taking our match over to a putt-putt over on Independence Boulevard. Now, we are talking rinky-dink miniature golf here—windmills, castle moats, banked shots, and all that crap. The reason I went with it was because I just couldn't see the guy beating me at any kind of golf, including miniature golf.

Obviously, he had had some experience with the "track," which I did not know. However, it didn't take me but a few times around to figure out all the rolls. I just focused in on the worn-out spots on the rails, aimed for those and relied on my feel. He really wasn't much of a putter anyhow, and before too long, he was into me for some serious "owesies." I brought up the subject of payment and he said that his only way out was to pay me with a number of checks, each one post-dated for the beginning of each month. I figured, what the hell and kept on playing. When he finally cried uncle about five in the morning, he owed me $11,000. He got out his checkbook and wrote me one current check for $1,000 and ten more like it.

Well, I guess it wasn't any surprise that that first check bounced. But what I couldn't believe, when I tried to run this deadbeat down, was that the guy had quit his job, just gone and pulled up and moved away. I couldn't get any leads on where he went and to this day, I never heard one word about anybody ever seeing him again. I've never played another game of miniature golf since then either.

There was a boy named Richard I used to play who worked for Wilson sporting goods. He was nice enough to play against, but again, he was one of these guys you never knew if you were going to get paid or not. If he had it, he'd pay; if he lost more than what he had on him, at least he'd empty his pockets for you. Lots of times, he wound up giving me equipment I couldn't really use, which I would either trade off or sell to somebody else. The trick with Richard was not to win too much money.

We were out at Eastwood one day, and Richard was getting himself stuck bad—$2,700. We got to the par-3 9th (we were only playing nine), and he wanted to play for the whole thing, one hole, double-or-nothing. I said, "You gotta' be nuts."

He said, "I thought you liked to gamble." Anyway, we dickered a bit and I offered to bet him $2,000 which he accepted. My reasoning was, I would let him win the hole and at least collect $700, maybe. There was just no point in having him owe me $5,400.

I knocked my shot into the trap on purpose; he got his on the edge of the green. I blasted out to where he was and figured I would just two-putt to make sure I lost. He three-putted and I had to do the same for a five to manage to drop the hole. Sometimes, people are just so intent on losing, it's tough to beat 'em to it. Anyway, Richard pulled out this huge wad, must have had $10,000 in it. "See what you could have won if you hadn't double-bogeyed," he laughed. I was sick— I had thrown off the hole and passed up $4,000. The next week, Richard was around and didn't even have money for greens fees.

In the late '70s, when I returned from a bad Vegas trip, I got a call from a high-rollin' gambler down in Alabama who wanted me to come play some golf. I was tapped out at the time and told him so. He said it didn't matter, that my marker was good and I could run a tab. He had a boy going on tour who he was backing, and he wanted to see how the kid would shape up playing against me. The boy didn't do well. I stayed a month and won $55,000—on the big guy's tab. Expenses about killed me, since I was half-broke to start with and had to borrow from home. When it was all over, the backer refused to pay me, claiming that the kid and I had "dumped him off."

That was outright imagination on his part, and I offered to take a lie detector test, but he wouldn't go for it. It was just his way out, that's all. Funny thing is, I'm protecting him right now by not using his name. Why?—because I might go down and play him or his horse again sometime. In my mind, I wrote it off. I won't ever get it and it won't ever be mentioned again. As far as I can see, it was just a case of me winning too much. We might bet again, but we damn sure won't play no tabs.

Here's another "tab" story. I was down in St. Pete, playing pool with a guy I'd met on the golf course. He couldn't bump it up fast enough, and it didn't take him long to lose the few hundred he had on him. It was one of my rare poolroom wins. He wouldn't let it go, and offered to put up his Caddy against $2,000. "Are you saying I can't win no cash?" I asked him. He told me that he would raise the cash for anything he lost, or else I would get the car.

I ended up winning $5,000 and wouldn't play for any more on the tab. He gave me the title and the keys. I left my car at the poolroom and drove the Caddy over to the Holiday Inn where I was staying. When I woke up the next morning, the Caddy was gone. That bastard had an extra set of keys, and when I looked down at the worthless replacement title he had given me, I realized he was still holding the original title. I never saw him again either.

There was another no-account I played with at Eastwood that nobody wanted any part of. Crazy Cole always found a reason to owe you money. It was all right with me though, 'cause he always seemed to pay me a little at a time. My trick was to make sure that I shorted what he owed me by fifty or a hundred. He thought he was getting over, but I knew what was going on all the time. "How come you always get paid, and Crazy Cole won't pay us?" people would ask me. "We just have a little agreement," I'd say.

One day Cole came up to me and had that, "I-got-a-deal-for-you look." "Leon," he asked me, "would you take $300 for that $600 I still owe you?"

"Hell yes," I told him. "Pay me."

"Nah, that's all right," he said. "But now I only owe you $300, right?"

9

Used, Borrowed, Bent, Stolen

The first clubs that I ever played with were whatever ones I could get my hands on around the caddy yard. There was a batch in the back of the shack in a big oak barrel, and one was just as bad as the next. It was first come, first served, and I remember how we all used to fight like alley cats for the five iron with the decent grip on it. Most of these old, wooden-shafted things were rusted out, crooked, and had worn-out grips on them. But every so often a decent club from the "lost and found" in the clubhouse would get lost and find its way to the barrel.

In our standard, two- or three-hole, one-club matches, you had to watch out for the boy with the premium stick; he's the one who would take down the dough that day. Otherwise, we were all pretty much swinging the same pipes, and they weren't any collectors' items either. But like I've mentioned before, that's how you learn to be a shotmaker, by playing the game over and over with just one club, any one club.

And if it looks like something out of a scrap iron yard, why that's all the better for your feel and touch in the long run.

After you experience caddy yard golf, once you do get some decent equipment in your hands, you feel like a world beater. Of course we didn't know that at the time and we just bashed the pill around with whatever we could latch onto.

The first full "matched" set of clubs I ever had, were ladies' clubs, the "Louise Suggs" model. They were a present from my daddy for my fifteenth birthday and I don't think he paid any notice to the name on the clubheads. They were only slightly used, but I can't imagine where he got them, since he was never anywhere nears a golf shop that I knew of. Maybe some woman golfer had left them behind in the trunk of one of his cabs.

I guess Louise Suggs was a pretty good player; she had to be to get her name on a line of clubs, since there sure weren't a lot of endorsements flying around in 1950. I took some ribbing for playing with "feminine" equipment, but it sure beat the hell out of anything else I'd ever used. And once I got to spanking the ball pretty good, people tended to forget what I was playing with. Ladies clubs are, of course, a bit shorter and usually more flexible in the shafts, but I couldn't really tell any difference, because, again, I didn't know any better. Anyway, we all know it's not the wand, it's the magician, right?

I played Louise for about a year—my game went from D- to B+ in that time. Then I got a big break from Clayton Heafner, who owned a piece of Eastwood. Heafner would get different new sets periodically from MacGregor, since he was one of the first "signature" pros who had hooked on with the company. (This was before Jack Nicklaus wound up owning about half the corporation, just for being Jack Nicklaus.) Whenever Heaf received a new batch, he took to leaving them with me to play with, so that I could "break in" the shafts.

He'd call me into his office and pull the clubs out of the long cardboard boxes they came in. Without even checking to see what new design they had come out with, he'd hand them to me and say, "Here, go loosen these up." I'd go play with them for a month or two until they were right for him. It was an honor around the club to get picked for this job, and I knew it was because he liked the way I banged the ball.

It was a matter of getting the shafts to where they would flex right. He'd feel them all along—sort of bend-test them— and when it got to where he liked them, he'd give me another set. Measuring flexibility in shafts was pretty much an inexact science more back then, compared to now. They sent him anything he wanted, and that's what I played with for a couple of years. From there I went to Spaulding, a club I used for a long, long spell. I played the old Spaulding Elite, the ones that all looked similar. From a two-iron to a wedge, all the heads appeared to be pretty much the same club—which is what appealed to me. That's something else about the equipment market. People are always stressing the importance of club fitting, and I agree. But whatever make or model club you might be shelling out those big bucks for, you had best make sure that hunk of metal at your feet looks right to you personally. Because if it doesn't, if it strikes you as too ugly design-wise, or it slants funny, whatever, you'll be wishing you hadn't laid your old set on the kid next door.

Those look-alike Elites also made it tough for my opponents to draw a bead on whatever club I was hitting with at any given time. I remember once, shortly after I'd bought them, when Cut-Shot Jerret watched me select and hit, then misclubbed himself and sent a three-iron flying twenty yards past a green into a nasty patch of Love Grass. I had hit a six-iron and I know he figured me for at least a four. He never said anything, but that bit of misinformation helped cost him that afternoon. Cut-Shot never did know what club to hit.

I banged those Elites about ten years, until I wore down the grooves on the short irons; I tried to find another set, but they had jazzed up the design ever so slightly, and they just weren't right for me. From there I went to the "Bird-on-Ball" Spaulding. There was a little round circle on the toe of the club, and it had a little birdie sitting on a ball. I hit those pretty sporty for about another ten years.

It's just amazing to see the choice of equipment available today. When I first started playing in the late '40s, it seems like there were maybe six, seven different sets you could find. Left-handers could pretty much forget about any selection, if they could find anything at all. Personally, I've enjoyed all of the changes. Over the years I've turned into a total freak for new sticks. As far as irons go, I'm a potential sucker for just about any kind of club, which I'm likely to turn over as quickly as I bought it. Mostly I'll just go by the clubhead; if it looks right, I'll take it, then go put the kind of shafts in that I'm used to playing with. Don't ask me what I'm using now, 'cause next week it's even money that I'll be changing over to something else.

I switched over from forged irons and wooden woods about two, three years after the cavity-backed irons and metal woods started getting popular. I figured everyone else was shootin' darts with the new equipment, I might as well try and do the same. What I did find out is that having always been a shotmaker, I couldn't hit what I call the "funny" shots with the new equipment. It sounds like a contradiction, but good players can't work the ball with the new like they could with the old, because the equipment is so much better. You just aim it down the middle of the fairway and it goes straight enough to hang your clothes on. Seems like there's something missing from the game; before you had to plan your shots a little more.

The exception is the new bubble shafts they've come up with. They have a big ole' knot up at the top, which seems to flex just right for me. I can work that shaft, draw or fade the ball, better than I can the old stuff. But with most of the other shafts nowadays, when I try to hit any kind of special shot, the ball wants to snap hook or slice. It's a fine edge, I guess.

Most serious golfers tinker with their golf clubs. From the years I spent working in a machine shop, I've always been pretty comfortable working on my sticks, getting them to where they look and feel right—personalizing the clubs. I don't have a basement workshop, but usually all I need is a vise to bend the suckers to where I like them.

Sometimes I'll seek out a loft-and-lie machine, if I want to get precise. That's an apparatus that pro and repair shops use to alter the degree of loft on the club, as well as the angle at which it lies. What I'm talking about here is the way the club lifts off the ground at the toe. I happen to like it a little flatter than most people, since I hit the ball high. By properly bending on the club hosel, the club can be "flattened out" which will allow for a lower trajectory.

The problem I'll often face is that I'll be in the middle of a round and the friggin' club just won't look right to me. It doesn't matter if the thing hasn't changed a millimeter since it left the factory or if I've played a hundred rounds with it, hit a thousand true shots, whatever—all of a sudden it just looks funny, the way the clubhead sits. So what do I do? Well I'll go for a little on-the-spot club adjustment right then and there.

Now a word of warning here. We all know the rules; or if you don't you should. How many times have you watched tour golf on TV and seen a guy finish a round putting with his driver. The reason? He somehow, usually in a fit of anger, bent or "altered" his putter so that it was not the same club that he had started the round with. In fact, here's the official United States Golf Association (USGA) rule:

"During a stipulated round, the playing characteristics of a club shall not be purposefully changed by adjustment or any other means."

So anyway, I'll just bang my club outright during a round of golf. And the way we play, nobody is going to call it. Or at least they'd better not, or they'll lose me. One of my favorite methods was with the old-time golf carts, the ones that had that big shock absorber on the back. I'd put the head down inside the spring and just push down on it and change it until I get it to sit and look right. I've done that many times.

Or if the cart doesn't have that spring—the new carts usually don't have those shackles, they've got hydraulic shocks—I'll look for an open pipe and use it like a vise.

Other times I've banged my club down on an old stump—just find a cut-down tree and bang the putter head on it. Whoever I'm playing with will think I'm all hot from blowing a putt and that now I'm taking it out on the club. Well, I've done that too, but in this case there's a method to my madness. Anybody who's playing with me on a regular basis will know that I'm just doing a little club adjustment.

Back in the days of wooden heads—remember them?—people I played with would commonly see me rubbing the shaft to get it warm, then putting it on my knee and just bending it near the hosel to get the head right. By getting the shaft warm, you could bend it without crimping it, but you can't do it with metal heads—they'll snap. Once, while I was playing a match up in the mountains, there was this guy who didn't know much about the game following us around, betting on my opponent. After he'd caught my bending routine a few times, he pulled his golfer over. "Hey man, why don't you try bending your damn clubs?" he said to him, and he was serious. "Leon's been doin' it all day, and he's beatin' you like a drum." The guy looked at him like he was nuts, and I about fell over.

Now, something else that can come up in the circles I play in, and that's when your clubs get adjusted for you, without you asking and without you knowing. That is not a good scene.

When I was out in Oklahoma, traveling with Titanic Thompson, I got a little surprise one morning that reminded me in a big way that I was out on the road, a long way from home. I had played this club pro on his turf, a semi-private course in Ardmore. It was deadly hot, but we got in twenty-seven holes before dark, with me a few hundred dollars winner. I was headed for our car, which was parked a couple hundred yards away, when my opponent called us over to the grill for a couple of drinks—on him.

Now, when you're on the road, and you are trying to beat somebody out of their money, you do not turn your back on hospitality. In fact, you remember that everybody's friends, and you take the time to enjoy company away from the battlefield. So my opponent seemed like a nice enough guy, so far.

We chatted for awhile, and as I was getting up to leave, my "host" said to me, "If we're going to play some more tomorrow, why don't you just leave your clubs here in the shop, that way you won't have to haul them back and forth in this heat." Well, I was dog-tired, and that seemed like a good idea. I said fine, thanked him and didn't think anything of it. It's not like I was going to go practice my swing in the motel room or anything.

Anyway, the next day, we met up with the guy, made the match—we had now jacked it up to $500 a side—and I went to get my clubs to bang some balls out on the range. My first few hits were pretty god-awful—they were sprayin' out like fireworks—which can always happen when you've just jumped out of the car. But then I realized the clubs didn't feel right and I immediately saw why. Someone had bent every damn club in my bag. The toes were standing way up off the ground. The five-iron was bent to almost a seven, the six-iron they had turned into a four, all the way down the line. I tried to figure each club out and try to gauge them accordingly, but there wasn't any pattern. I mean they had done one masterful job of messing up my sticks.

When Ti stopped by the practice tee—as usual, to check out my swing—I told him, "Ti, they have done went and ruined my clubs."

He said, "Let me see," and picked a three-iron out of the bag. He looked at it like he was a jeweler or something, although you really didn't have to examine them up close. He looked up at me with this twinkle in his eye, like he could appreciate their attempt at getting the big edge, even if it was sort of lame. I mean, how would any decent golfer not know what was up? "You gotta' be kidding," he said.

"Well, there's only one thing I can do," I said, "and that's go buy a new set of clubs." Ti hated digging for expense money, and he knew that any new equipment was going to come at least half out of his pocket.

"See if they won't give you a discount," he said.

I didn't ask for any discount, and I didn't try for a trade-in either. I popped for a new set of Spauldings that beat the hell out of my old ones, and I remember the assistant-pro behind the register looking all-the-way guilty. But the best of all was when I got to the 1st tee, where my opponent was waiting. I took those old clubs and made a big show of dumping them out in a small chicken wire trash bin they had at the side of the tee box. "I guess I won't have any use for these any-more," I told him with a big smile on my face.

He didn't say a word, didn't pretend like I shouldn't be throwing away good clubs, or anything. In fact, he was kind of quiet the whole round. It's hard to talk when you're drowning, which he was, to the tune of the $2,000 in green we wound up taking down—minus the cost of new sticks.

*   *   *

Of course, like most hotheads, I've busted my share of clubs just by getting a little too out of sorts. I've never been much of a club thrower—I might like to fling it down sometimes—but I have been a buster. I broke a lot of drivers over the years; seems like every time I did, it was always my best one and I'd be really sorry about it later.

Down in Florida once, I split the shaft on this blonde persimmon driver after an ugly snap hook—broke it right across my knee. I can remember regretting it as I was doing it. Anyway, I must have changed the shaft a half dozen times trying to get one I really liked. Each time you do that the neck on the club gets a little shorter from working it down to make it fit. So the last time I reshafted it, I knew I was about out of room and couldn't be breaking that club any more. The end result was that I wound up playing with the club for a long time.

What with his temper and all, Tommy "Thunder" Bolt had a reputation for being pretty hard on his clubs. There's a famous photo taken of him flinging his driver into a lake at the U.S. Open, at Cherry Hills. But in all the rounds we played, I never did see him break or throw a club. He did, however, have a pet saying that made pretty good sense: "If you're going to throw a club, make sure you release it in front of you. That way, you won't hit anybody, and you won't have to walk back to pick it up."

If you've got to go that way, the safest way to break a club is across the knee, but you can still get hurt. My partner Dickie snapped a shaft once, and the jagged end wound up sticking him right square in the kneecap. We had to carry him to the hospital. Down at Myrtle Beach I saw a guy try to wrap a five-iron around a tree. The shaft bounced off of the tree and stuck him in the chest like a spear. If I'm gonna' do anything I make sure that it will be to my leg or something. It's really pretty dumb, though, when you think, "it can't be me, it's got to be the golf club."

You know those suede head covers that let everybody know you're playing the world's most expensive golf clubs? Do yourself a favor and chuck those in the trunk and get an old woolly cover, a monkey-head, anything. Otherwise, you are a sitting duck to get thieved. Believe me, I know. I get parking lot offers to buy and sell clubs every day of the week; some of 'em are hot enough to melt the pavement I'm standing on.

The very favorite club I ever owned was lifted from my bag a few years back, and I'll tell you, it just about ruined my game. It wasn't an expensive item in the usual sense, but it was priceless as far as I was concerned. It was just an old Tony Penna sand wedge, but it had a couple thousand rounds of my personalized feel grooved into it.

At one time I was a sensational wedge player, and that club was like an extension of my arms. From sixty yards in, I truly felt that I was going to hole every shot, when I had it in my hands. For a few years, I was probably up-and-down 80 percent from that distance.

Well, it may be coincidence, but my wedge play has deteriorated steadily since the day that club was stolen. Today, it's the worst part of my game—for a lot of different reasons, mostly my wrists. I've probably played a couple hundred different wedges since I lost my Tony Penna, but none of them ever approached the "feel" of that particular club. I put out a

$500 reward at the time, but I didn't hear a peep out of any-body. I've always had a sneaking suspicion that whoever was responsible had a lot more at stake than that in seeing me minus my magic wand.

Yes, the reward offer still stands.

10

Partners

No matter how much full-bore gamble or lights-out golf talent I've had, I never could have survived the way I have without partners. When you get around high-dollar games, playing with a partner is somedays the only action you're going to find. Backers, people who put up the money, like to play, too. Teams match play is one surefire way to get everybody involved, and it can turn into a great equalizer as well.

There aren't that many scratch golfers who are looking to bet other scratch golfers head up, and there aren't that many hackers looking to gamble, either. That's why all the dickering over strokes and how you're going to play—if you ever in fact do play—can about ruin a nice sunny morning. But if I say, "Tell you what, I'll take ole' Shank Watkins over here, against you and Banana Slice Stevens," everybody's purse strings might loosen up a bit. You've got to be careful though, since you're no longer strictly on your own. Choosing a partner can be an inexact science, but you had best learn it if you want to be successful, and if you want to stay friends with the people you tee it up with and against.

*   *   *

One of the finest partners I've ever been hooked up with is a local boy from Charlotte named Dickie Starnes. We began playing together over twenty-five years ago at Eastwood. Dickie took up the game in his twenties; at the time, he was a perfect partner for my caliber, since you need a weaker player to get the games. Only Dickie was never truly a weaker player, though at times he may have looked like one. He could sneak up on people by shooting 76 without hitting but maybe three, four greens in regulation the entire round. People often judge a player by what happens off the tees and down the fairways, but Dickie putted and chipped so well that it made all the difference. We ran together for years and made some pretty good money along the way.

The most important skill to look for in a good sidekick is having someone who can putt. You can teach anybody to hit the rock, but it's hardly any use if he can't clear the table. Dickie grooved his game on par-3 golf and became a good wedge player that way. He couldn't hit all that long, but he was arrow-straight down the runway. I knew that with his sound fundamentals, it was just a matter of time and experience before he'd be an all-around player. In the meantime, up-and-down was the name of his game. But he's worked so much on his game over the years that it's gotten near the point that when we team up nowadays, we've about switched roles and I'm the helper.

Another benefit to a good partnership is personality. Of course, the two of you have to hit it off, which probably isn't a problem if you're still teamed up after a few rounds. But beyond that, your partner has to know how to handle himself—on the course and off it, too. Dickie was always pretty sporty at the 19th hole—gracious win or lose. You've got to have the right attitude if you want to hang onto the game. You can't get to crying if things don't roll your way, and you can't get too cocky with a few lucky bounces.

For the better part of one summer, Dickie and I had a game going with Mark Gooden and Bobby Bridges, a couple of top Carolina players. Counting presses, we played that you could win or lose around $800 if someone was goin' good or bad. One day we were playing at the Links of Tryon, and up a few hundred, when Mark made some comment to Dickie like, "Oh, y'all probably quit us after this." It kind of took us by surprise since the game was even and friendly.

Dickie fired right back. "We'll never quit." Not only that, he offered them a $10,000 "contract," whereby nobody could quit until somebody was up or down the $10,000. They accepted and we battled for a couple of months until one day Mark pulled up, stuck $9,200. They paid up and Dickie said to me, "You think I ought to tell them there's still $800 to go?"

"Don't you dare say a word," I told him.

Bob Bryant partnered with me a few times, and as tough a player as he was, I just had to let it go. Besides being just about the saddest piss-and-moan loser I ever saw, he was worse than diarrhea as a winner. It wasn't enough to drum somebody out of their money, he had to run his mouth and degrade people. "You can't play," he would yammer at some guys we had just been beaten out of a week's salary. "You ain't got no business even playing for ten cents."

I would tell him to leave it alone, but he wouldn't be stopped. "That just makes them want to play more," he would tell me. I knew it didn't. Nobody needs to be ribbed or knocked after they just handed over the dough. It's more like, who needs this crap? Finally, we began to lose our opponents on that effect, because it happened so many times. "Why the hell do you want to play with him?" people would ask me over and over, which finally made me realize I'd better get away. So I did.

"Captain's Choice" is a game we play a lot of, and it's basically a "scramble" format where everybody will hit and teams will play off the best shot. The teams may vary in combinations. It may be me and one other player against four, five guys, or it may be a standard two-against-two, or sometimes we'll go off an eightsome, four-against-four. Handicaps are virtually unheard of in these games. Basically, the handicapping amounts to what kind of players you're teamed up with. You might have one scratch golfer partnered with a 10 handicap against, say, three 5- or 6-handicappers. You try to equal everybody up and make it as close as possible, but it doesn't always work out that way.

Unlike "best ball," where the single best score on a team wins the hole, in Captain's, two good players might just run over you if your partner can't help out a lick. If he can't hit a drive, an approach, or sink a putt, you'll end up using all of your shots and none of his. You've got no room for mistakes. Meanwhile, two good players, pooling their talents, can come up with enough good shots to beat you—if you're never getting any help, that is.

I've had one character—a friend I'll call Tommy, since I don't want to embarrass him—down here in Charlotte, who always wanted to take me for a partner. He'd call me up and say, "I'm off today, let's go get 'em"—meaning let's go bet a bunch of money and Leon can bail us out. I'd actually rather have him on the other side. He's a super guy who will bet anything, with anybody, at any given time; that's just the problem. He's too jumpy and would get us in a trap in no time at all. "Let's feel this out first," I'd tell him when he'd start chomping at the bit.

"We'll kill 'em," he'd say. After some of the games he'd made, I knew the only way we'd kill anybody is by choking them to death on our money.

One game that neither of us will ever forget was when Tommy and I played Captain's against three scratch golfers out at Cedarwood for a sizable nassau. Now Tommy's about a 10 handicap on a good day, and this wasn't one of his better ones. I don't think he cut me any shots the entire round. On the course, the man is something else to behold, long hair flowing like Custer, his lady riding alongside him in the golf cart, gun sticking out of his back pocket—just way too much. Anyway, I'm carryin' all the weight, up against it and playing the 9th hole, a 247-yard monster par 3, into the wind. If I don't par, we're probably out at least $5,000, solid losers. Everybody missed the green, and I just crushed a four-wood, four feet from the pin. I sank the birdie putt to get us even, and about duplicated the feat on the 18th, needing a miracle five-wood up-and-down from 230 yards to save the back nine. Tommy whooped it up pretty good, and he still does every time he brings it up. Those two shots saved us $10,000—we broke even—but we never should have been in that spot to begin with.

*　　*　　*

105

One of the darker sides to team play, especially when you get around some desperate people, is the fine art of dumping. And believe me, it is a fine art, for it can happen right under your nose, and you still might be the last person to smell the rat. Anything can happen when you are picking partners out of a hat, on a strange course, and out of town. But I've been dumped on by golfers I trusted, and that makes it all the worse.

The first time I ever came face to face with that kind of larceny was when I was playing Floren Depaglia, who was a pretty well-known golf hustler in the '60s. Depaglia came through Charlotte a few times and didn't fare so well. But he did scare me half to death the day he walked over to me during a round, and brought up what is more politely referred to as "doing business." I remember it clearly, since I was standing over a ball that had wound up on some gravel around a drainpipe. We were playing everything "down"—no relief anywhere, which is a way to play when nobody trusts each other.

"Boy, you're crazy anyway," he said to me, talking out of the side of his mouth, so none of the eyeballers could hear. "You can make a lot more money losing than you can by winning. Everybody on this course bets on you, know what I mean? You wouldn't have to ever worry about shots like this or where your ball winds up."

I was at a total loss for words. The idea that somebody wanted me to double-cross my own friends shook me up so bad I couldn't hit a ball for the rest of that day.

When I was still young and, I guess, still green, I got involved in a game where I partnered with a truck company owner against a couple of regulars at Eastwood. The game was tough, maybe a little bit in our favor, and we wound up a slight winner. The losers called me up the next day and asked me to come on out for the same game. When I got there, they told me the trucking man had to go out of town, but they had another partner for me. I said fine, 'cause frankly, I felt like I could carry anybody, no matter how much a load they put on me.

The problem was, I couldn't carry a dumpster. They beat "us" out of $3,100, which was just a ton of money to me back then. I figured we'd flat out lost on the square, although I couldn't understand how my partner, who was normally a conservative putter, could run so many twelve-footers four feet by the hole. "What's goin' on, man?" I would ask him. "The speed of these greens has got me all confused," was the best that he could come up with.

Anyway, about five years later, one of the vultures on the other side had an argument with one of the others, and he came and fessed up to me about how all three of them had set me up. He explained that they were really after the trucking guy's money, but as long as I was around, their game was in trouble. So they had to get me out of the way, and that was the only way they knew how.

After hearing that, I got real dedicated to going after the other two, which I did the only way I knew how—with my sticks. It took me a while, but I trapped 'em in games they couldn't pass on, then I just scorched 'em. I was so inspired that I scalded that damn course with some of the best golf I have ever played. Afterwards, I got the cutthroats together, bought them a drink, and told them that I knew what they'd done. They got all apologetic and told me they never expected me to pay up, that they just wanted me away from their action and figured that I would stay clear if I owed them money. Well, I half-bought their convoluted story, but I didn't really care so much by that point. I knew I wasn't dealing with any choirboys, but I took it as a lesson and swore to be more cautious. It can still happen.

Sometimes a dump-job can be pretty transparent. A partner I had down in Florida once missed a four-inch putt on the 8th hole. Four inches! The "yips" can get you anytime but not at that distance. I mean, try and miss that length putt—it's near impossible, unless you whiff altogether or go and hit it in the other direction. We were playing for $1,500 and that tap-in was to square up the match. He stubbed a two-footer on the 9th hole for insurance, but I still could have saved my end with a birdie. Hell, my mind was so blown, I bogeyed the hole. I quit, paid up, and split.

I have to confess to having bet the correct side on games that I suspected weren't on the level. There was a high-roller down in Myrtle Beach who was very unpredictable about his golf. He might throw off a game for spite, just to make a side bettor lose if he didn't like that person. One time I was at the Beach with Charlie Miller, a friend from Charlotte, when we spotted this guy at the Robber's Roost course, setting up some hotshot locals against a couple of outsiders who had to be clear underdogs. Everybody loved the homers so we took the other guys, which we figured was where the main man's interests lied.

We guessed right and won the bet, but it wasn't without a scare. On the 9th hole, one of the local pros hit his shot out of the trap; it looked like he was trying to fly it way over the green. The ball came out too low, hit the top of the flagstick, and dropped straight down into the cup for a bird to win the front. With all the local money riding, you'd have thought these guys had just copped the Masters. Anyway, we just doubled our bets, and it worked out all right in the end for us. Thankfully, those snakes made sure they didn't hit anymore "lucky" shots all day.

I partnered some with Marshall Carpenter, a pool hustler known as "The Squirrel," more for his abilities to find good games than for his golfing skills. Squirrel was about a 10 handicap, but he had a nose for money. One time, he had heard about a man down in Meridian, Mississippi named Council Hightower who had inherited some money and loved to play golf. We headed down there with the understanding that Council would have a partner and we would play best ball matches.

At the driving range at the Meridian Country Club, it took me about two seconds to see who the other partner was. There were about twenty golfers hitting balls, but only one of them had the perfect golf swing. He turned out to be Mike Taylor, the state amateur champion and a teammate of Johnny Miller's at Brigham Young University.

We were playing their home course at terrible odds, but then again, how could they, or even I, know that I would choose that time to play some of the best golf there ever was? I shot so well out of the gate the first couple of days, that it threw off their timing—they never got a chance to feel like the favorites. There was a 400-yard, dogleg finishing hole that I played totally wrong by flying directly over all the trouble, but I felt totally bulletproof.

After about ten days, we, or rather, I started to tail off a bit, and the game showed itself to be plenty tough. But they'd had enough, and I truly felt that even though we were $18,000 winners, we had escaped a major trap. I also think Council bet so much on ball games, that this golf gambling was like playing for fun. As for Squirrel, he set up the game, we escaped, and he didn't really have to do anything else but watch.

As much gamble as I've got, there have been a few times when I felt it best to pull up. If you're with a partner, bucking 2–1 against, and you get a chance for an out, you've got to take it. That's the way it happened for me once when I was playing a $10,000 match at Cleghorne, a bear of a mountain course.

I was teamed with Chip Fasmeier who, even if he was a short hitter, surely did help me out on a few holes. But coming into the long par-5 18th hole, we were all even and in an iffy situation. We could win or lose the ten, or break even. The hole did not set up well for Chip—for anybody, really. The fairway ran mostly downhill, but you had to try and reach a far-off plateau area, if you wanted to get up over a lake that fronted the green. From a downhill lie, flying the lake was damn-near impossible and reaching the green was out-of-the-question.

The hole was a bitch, no doubt about it, but it surprised me that our opponents brought up "offing" the bet, as we were getting ready to hit. They were both pretty long hitters, yet they made the offer, which didn't go over too well with all the eyeballers who had been sweatin' and bettin' all the way and wanted to see some kind of finish. Chip didn't care what we did, but he knew that the hole was squarely on my shoulders. I felt that too many things could go wrong, so I accepted to halve the match, and we all walked in. If I'd had a little more support, I'd a gone for it. But after that offer had been made, I felt like I'd be a real fool if we wound up losing. Sometimes you just got to kiss that sister and forget about it.

11

Loose Money

Gambling money has no home. That's an old saying we have down here, and I want to tell you I've proved it out countless times. You won't find too many gamblers who visit the bank on any regular basis. The bankroll might get nice and fat for awhile, but then, just as sure as little green apples, it'll start thinning out again. It's really an unavoidable part of the action life, unless you're a total locksmith. Hit the slide, tap out, go borrow some money, and start all over. The idea is pay some bills when you get a chance, make sure the family's set for awhile, and try and hang on.

One major problem with staying well is that betting doesn't just end at the golf course; it never did, and it didn't start there either. There's just so many things that can happen to get any kind of gambler parted from his cash. Golf happens to be my angle, and I do well at it. People who like to bet on it used to generally pass the money along to me; thing is, I've always had at least a half-dozen or so ways to pass it back.

*   *   *

Dice hypnotize people, at least they do me. I can say right now that if I see 'em I won't mess with 'em, but deep down inside, I know better. I'm a sucker for a craps game. There's been a few times that I've been very lucky, but more often than not, it's been the other way around. If you could tally it all up, I know I'd have been better off if I'd never touched the cubes.

I've run into some pretty big dice games around golf courses. The temptation is to dip in and get your feet wet, see if you can get in on a roll and tap into some serious cash. But it is hypnotizing. Let's say that I need to make either a six or an eight, I'll start getting that dread fear, because I just know like a dead cinch that a seven is coming—just flat out know it. When it does, I'll keep playing. The dice will make you find money you don't even know you have, then send you out to borrow more. And I'm also talking games on the square; if I feel that anything's funny about a game—and you get plenty of those—I won't go near it.

In Vegas, you have to watch out for what we call "maneuverers." You pal up with a guy, and he'll say, "let's go partners, $500 apiece, see if we can win us somethin'." The deal here is, you're each supposedly playing a $500 stake, with the understanding that you'll split up any winnings. Before you know it, you're stuck five bills and wind up digging a deeper hole trying to get it back, and that's the name of that game. Forget the other guy, he was shilling for the house and he's long gone. His job was just to get you to the crap table in the first place.

There was a game on the front porch at Eastwood, in 1972, going on most of the afternoon. I was holding up all right, then I had to leave to go home and get dressed for a date I had that night. Around seven o'clock, I was driving back by the golf course towards my dinner date, when I looked over and saw the cars still there. I figured, what the hell, let me just get a couple of rolls in.

I pulled up to the game, just for a momentary action stop, even left my car door open. I was holding the dice, about to make my second roll, when a hand grabbed my arm. The hand belonged to a sheriff, and the game was getting popped. These things used to happen sometimes around election time. Anyway, they cuffed all seven or eight of us, took us all downtown and locked us up. I had to get bailed out by a friend and wound up paying a twenty-five-dollar fine. Needless to say, I never made that date. It's the only time I've ever been in a jailhouse, and I don't ever care to visit another. It's a funny sound when those steel bars clang shut—kind of reminds you of the movies.

But a little success will keep you coming back to any kind of action. About thirty years ago, I blew my last twenty-eight dollars in a crap game. Jack Horton, who was then the Eastwood assistant pro, loaned me a few bucks to get back in, and little-by-little, I got hotter than a sun spot—I wound up busting everybody in the whole damn game. When it was all over I had cash spilling out of every pocket. I literally couldn't find places to stash it. Best of all, I had won Catfish's Cadillac Seville—traded him for my Ford Falcon to even up for what he owed me.

James Black was in the game, and watched Catfish and I exchange auto titles. "Damn, Catfish," he said. "I know you done gone plum crazy. Any man would trade a Caddy for a Ford ain't got the sense of an earthworm."

*　　*　　*

The dogs are another big potential drain; you don't see too many people getting rich at dog tracks. I never did get a whole lot of enjoyment watching a bunch of hounds chase an electric rabbit. It was just a way to kill some time away from the golf course, also a surefire way to lighten up the ole' pocket. But the last time I got stung, I got cured.

I was in Florida in '75, teaming up with Bill Harvey, a good player from Greensboro. Funny, you can go partners with somebody and you might be impressed with the way they handle themselves on the course. Then you go out at night together and see a whole other person. "Let's bet the dogs together," he says to me, like we're gonna spend a few dollars and have some fun.

Next thing I know, he's at the fifty-dollar window, having the lady hold the damn button down until the race starts. Hey, I'm in halves with him! After about three races, my cash was gettin' funny. He'd had a couple of drinks and was getting kind of jumpy. He was just betting way too much on the dogs, and I didn't like the spot I was in. The odds, of course, were dropping down to even money with every bet he made. I backed off a considerable loser, but I kept tabs on Bill—he didn't hit a pooch all night, and I haven't bet on one since.

Now, there is an exception to every rule, and I knew a guy around St. Pete who was always beating the dogs. The trouble was, he never shared his information. We called him Big Bob, 'cause he always hit it big. His thing was to watch about ninety-nine races a week without making a play, then send it all in. He bet maybe three times total in a week and actually studied every race on every card. I heard he wound up beating the IRS on some famous tax case. He claimed he was a professional gambler and had every expense itemized—down to pencils, car depreciation, everything. It will never cease to amaze me how some people earn a living.

Bookmaking is about the most common profession I know of in my circles. Seems like bookies are always around making themselves available should you want to wager on anything from a ballgame to a cockroach race. Here in North Carolina, of course, you have your major sports betting, but you also have a lot of action on pro golf and NASCAR. To me, flipping a coin is a far sight better than betting race cars since you got thirty, forty automobiles can knock you out at any given time—clip a fender and you're out.

The way golf betting works down here is a book will put out a line that pairs off different tour golfers for one round only in a tournament. You can pick one golfer against another, but you're laying 6–5 odds on the money. I'll never forget the time that I had bet Fred Couples over Tom Kite in first day of play at the Greater Greensboro Open. Couples was about six shots better with nine holes to go, and he blew it—for my purposes anyway. That's when I realized I couldn't even pick my nose.

You're supposed to feel safe with a six-shot lead, nine holes to go, but when you think about it, it's really not that much. Player A can shoot 32 and player B can shoot 38—simple as that. Professionals are all capable of shooting 30 anytime they tee up, just like they can blow up to 37, just as easy. So many times my "horse" would have a two-, three-shot lead with two, three holes left, and I'd think, hey, this looks good. Next thing I knew I was in the dungeon.

There is one guy I know, Eddie the Chicken Man, who

seems to make out pretty good all the time. Eddie called me up from Augusta one year when they still had that big Calcutta pool— that's where they auction off golfers, the money goes into a common pot, and they pay off first, second, third, etc. Anyway, Eddie had bought Larry Mize at what he thought was a bargain price and wanted to know if I wanted any piece of it.

I said "Larry Mize? What the hell are you tryin' to lay off on me?" Well, Mize made that famous chip-in over Greg Norman in sudden death to win the Masters that year and Eddie pulled down a huge chunk of money on a few hundred dollar investment. But that's Eddie. One time he got into a hole-in-one contest in Vegas at the last minute—had to beg 'em to take his five dollars. He knocked the rock in the hole for a new Buick. I've had seventeen holes-in-one, and all I ever got was an ashtray with a Titleist ball mounted in the middle.

Sports betting is a stone killer. I swear, I wished to hell I never ever bet a single game in my life. I was in Florida one winter when I called home one day and a good friend told me about a tout they had who was picking ninety percent on basketball—a sport I hardly ever messed with. I said sounds good, and asked him to give me his picks. I bet thirteen games that night and for some reason I couldn't get the results. Around 11:30, I called my friend and asked how we did. He told me to read off my teams, since he had gone and bet a few more games. I called off the first six, and they were all losers. I figured, well, maybe the last six or seven will be winners. The seventh was a push, or tie, and the last six were losers. I was sick.

I talked to my friend a few days later and asked him if his

man was doing any better with the ball. "Yeah," he told me. "He's back to pickin' winners."

"Is that right?" I said. "He done picked me out."

Football, as every bettor knows, can be just as brutal. I've had a lot of bad beats, but the one I remember best was the Giants against the Raiders on a Monday night game. I had already bet the Raiders, and there were about ten of us hanging out at Eastwood, when we all decided to pool some money on a pick service. I told them before the call that I knew what their pick would be, and of course, it was Giants. "Well, what do we do now cuz?" I asked a fellow Raiders bettor.

He said, "We paid to get this tip, we'd better jump the fence."

Which we did, to the Giants. I think the final score was 37–0 Raiders. So much for the pick service. I had plunged over $2,000 on the game, and I had to sell a nice little El Camino I had at the time to pay the man. Jumping sides is the best way I know to get rid of your cash. I lost my wheels and everything else on that one, but that's the way it goes— first your money, then your clothes.

In a lot of places, playing gin rummy is what you do after you're done with a day of golf. The cards can stretch out anywhere from an hour or two, on into the night. While I do play at it, I'm not all that much of a gin player. Of course I try to come out on top, but if I'm looking like an underdog, I generally try to hand back just part of the money I've won and not all of it.

Sitting down for gin is a courtesy of my profession. It's not like I can say, "No, you're a better gin player," or "I really don't feel like playing." People always want to have a chance to get their money back and it's usually at gin. But you can't be a sucker, because the pace is one hell of a lot faster than a round of golf. If you can't hold your own and manage yourself, you're in trouble. And if you flat out refuse to play, you can wave your golf game bye-bye birdie.

Now, time can be a very important factor especially as far as momentum swings. We all know that cards run hot and cold. If I am winning in a gin game—I definitely do not want to be there all night. Also, when I hear somebody say, "We'll call it at seven o'clock," I know that's a joke, too. What I try to do is be firm, not look at the clock, just get up and say, "Time for me to go."

I have played in gin games that were not on the level, which is bad enough for a good player. In Michigan, I was playing three-man gin with a Mafia guy I'd beaten on the course, and I knew something was funny. I didn't know whether the other guy was a card mechanic (they'd have to be pretty bad for me to catch them) or whether they had signals—I just have a sixth sense when something is wrong. So I just stalled best I could, threw away lots of high cards, and hung on for dear life. After I felt I'd spent enough time, I just said I had to go—no excuses, just "gotta go."

Speaking of which, there was some real, low-down gin cheating going on down in Florida at some of the Miami clubs I played. I remember two boys who had a code of words that represented all of the cards. "Well" was the Ace, "come" was the King," "get" was the Queen, and so on, down the line. They had the whole deck covered. One of them would be out of the game—sitting, watching, and making casual conversation; at the same time he was identifying another guy's cards to his partner across the table. Some cheats love to brag, and the guy had explained his whole system to me after a few drinks one night.

Also, around that scene down there, in the '60s, there was a hustlers' code that applied to just about any con that people might have going. If you were to spot somebody cheating somebody else at cards, whatever, or even golf, you could give the cheat the "I-want-in-on-your-action" signal, which was shown by an open palm across the chest. If the guy answered you with the same signal, then you knew that he would cut you in on his score later on. If he answered with a closed fist on the chest, that meant you were out, and it was your call if you wanted to let the sucker know what was up—sometimes at your own peril, of course.

There are plenty of strictly gin hustlers around and you have to watch out for them, too. Golf, for them, is just an excuse to get to the card table. Here you've got to be careful of the guy who won't bet much over four hours of golf, but wants to jack it up high when you get over a deck of cards in the clubhouse.

I, myself, once had a gin game that I couldn't wait to get to. The man was an airline pilot named Bob, who, about fifteen years ago, used to come out to Paradise Valley when he wasn't flying. To be quite frank, I could have dispensed with the golf entirely—that's how bad he was at gin, especially once he started drinking. But he wouldn't play gin unless he lost on the golf course, or at least lost say, $1,000. That just motivated me even more to beat him at golf. Funny thing, he wasn't all that bad a golfer. But he could not put a hand together at cards—the man played gin like he was playing Old Maid or something. I sure wish Bob was in town right now.

12

On the Road, Again

As much as I can't stand to be away from home, the road does make for some interesting situations. If you're gonna be a hustler—and I'm not talking about someone who takes advantage of people, I'm talking someone who can raise his game to meet every occasion—then you've got to cut your teeth on different sets of circumstances. If you're any kind of real player, you'll find it out by teein' up away from home—away from your rooters and away from the course where you know every bump and roll, every blade of grass, and every spike mark. Lots of players do real well at home—I always did, myself. But take them out on the road and watch 'em wilt. You've got to be able to stand the heat, and there's no shortage of heat out there.

There's stuff that can happen to you when you travel to different golf courses that you just wouldn't believe. Paid-off greens keepers will usually serve up home cooking that, guaranteed, will give you indigestion. I've always been a hooker, so it's no surprise when I get into a game and the pins are all set on the right side of the greens where it's all that much harder for me to get close to the hole. Other times, the cups can be just a little raised up without you realizing it, so's if you try and die the ball in the hole instead of hitting it firm, it'll just roll off. Once when I was in Oklahoma, they had the flags in the confoundest places, usually blind spots where I couldn't see the trouble until it was too late. I'd try and flag the ball, and just when I thought I'd dropped a dart, I'd find my ball in a deep, drop-off bunker no more than fifteen feet from where the cup was cut. Of course my opponent would be safely on. I've even heard of them moving the yardage markers around, which would damn sure throw most people.

Eyeballers can be pretty cold on the road, too. You'll hear all kinds of comments, things like, "he's really in jail there," when you're in a little trouble, or "he can't possibly get home from there," when you're looking at a long distance call from a buried lie—just little things to work on your mind. You can't react or it'll get worse. You've got to eat it and let your sticks do the talking.

Probably the toughest road contest I ever took on was back in the late '60s on the plains of West Texas against a boy who was the finest ball striker I ever saw. (When I saw him recently, he told me that he wanted no part of this, so we'll just call him Billy.) I was with Titanic Thompson looking for games in that area, and we knew in advance about Billy; Ti called him the best golfer in the world, at the time. The idea was to play anybody *except* him, but that's not how it worked out.

Billy was only twenty-one or twenty-two years old and fixing to go on the tour. At the same time, he had a handful of gamblers betting on him and backers staking him against all comers. Everything about his game was so pure; there were no flaws to it, and, like me, he felt like he could do anything with a golf ball. On his home turf, he was stronger than rent.

After Ti couldn't find me any other games, he set me up with Billy on what I recall was a long and scraggly public layout. We were playing medal (best score) for $2,500, and what stands out most in my memory was my opponent lighting up the back nine with seven straight birdies. Hell, I shot six under par and lost by two strokes to a 63. That track stretched out like miles and miles of lonesome road, and he just jumped all over it.

Ti didn't want me to tackle Billy anymore—said that we'd made a big mistake, which kind of hurt my feelings. So, I got up the next day and told Ti I wasn't going to leave town without trying him one more time. And besides, I figured the boy just couldn't shoot back-to-back rounds like that. I was wrong—he could, and he almost did, until something very lucky for me happened to turn things around.

We played that second time—again for $2,500—this time at the local country club, which was truly Billy's backyard, and where he figured to have an even stronger edge than he had the previous day. But what I didn't know was that his father was a high-faluttin' member there, and that he didn't want his son involved in anymore gambling action. We were all even mid-way through the back nine when the old man got word of what was going on out on the course. He pulled up in a cart on the 16th tee and tore into his son. "Didn't I tell you I didn't want you gambling anymore?" he yelled. "If I ever catch you gambling again, you're not getting a penny from me to go on tour. Is that clear? Make up your own mind what you want to do."

I could see the son was getting visibly upset, so I just sat back and waited it out; this was all very good for my end. I think I saw Ti wink at me as the daddy was carryin' on. Meanwhile, the bettors and sweators had considerable change riding on the match; the boy was of age and couldn't just go home with his tail between his legs. He tried reasoning with the old man saying, "Dad, I'm not bettin' nothin'. They're all bettin' on me—I'm just playing."

The father didn't want to hear about it—"I don't want you involved with gambling in any way."

Well, we played it out, but Billy couldn't concentrate much after that, and I got him by three strokes. I don't know how it would have come out otherwise, but I was certainly glad for that interruption. We never played again. I know Billy did have a few years on tour, but I heard that he ran into some severe problems with his back and had to give it up. Man, he was some player.

Like just about anybody who's bet serious money on golf, I've spent my share of time in Las Vegas. But I never really made out all that well there. For a gambling town, the golf action is anything but loose—some of these guys will hold on for dear life before parting with any scratch. I guess they're all saving it for the tables. There have been a few major scores—poker champ Doyle Brunson beat a drug dealer headed for jail out of several hundred thousand dollars at the Las Vegas Country Club one afternoon in the late '80s—but as far as my action was concerned, I wasn't breaking any banks.

Out in Vegas, they don't really care that much if you make

a golf game or not. There's so much overall traffic out there that they know if it's not you, it's going to be somebody else—there's fresh meat all the time. Also, they're *at* home and they know you're *away* from home. Already you're battling expenses and casino losses, so they can try and get you out of line. Before you know it, you'll find yourself in a tough game, say, giving up too many strokes to a good player, when you really shouldn't. That's happened to me many a time.

When anybody finally does make a game, they treat money like dirt. I played with Brunson, Puggy Pearson, Chip Reese, and Billy Baxter, all top poker players and excellent golf handicappers. You won't find too many players in Vegas who claim to be a 5 handicap when they're actually a 10—usually you'll run into the opposite. And about your own game, well, they've already made the phone calls and done all the research to find out exactly how you really do play. They leave nothing to chance.

A few times I played in an annual golf hustlers' match-play tournament run by Jack Binion, owner of the Horseshoe Casino. This was an event that welcomed bookies, gamblers, and golfers from all over the country. It also featured some bending of traditional golf rules. You were allowed to use Vaseline or grease on your clubs—it keeps the ball from hooking or slicing—and if people could get away with cheating any other way, they just went ahead and did it.

Probably the toughest thing to overcome was the handicapping, which wasn't all that legitimate. There was a great deal of side-betting on all the matches, and everybody was looking for inside information—mainly whose handicap was accurate and whose wasn't. I lost in the finals one year to one of Amarillo Slim's boys mainly because I had to overspot him. But everybody did generally have a good time in this late-summer tournament, which was kind of like a busman's holiday for all the bookies, before they went back to work for the football season.

One of the highlights of my golfing life was the time I spent around Dean Martin in Vegas. Club singer Don Cherry, who once played the golf tour, one day asked me if I'd like to play a friendly round with Dean. I said sure, he set it up, and Dean and I hit it off pretty good.

Dean loved his golf, and I know he enjoyed playing with me. I gave him five, six shots a side, and I think I beat him, all told, out of fifty dollars over two days—not that I was looking to score. He had a decent swing which was amazing, considering he had a drink in his hand no matter what time of the day it was. He seemed to order a different cocktail every time, and it sure kept him loose as a goose. If he had a care in the world you would never know it; he'd be singing and humming his way up and down the fairway.

Dean took a liking to me and invited me to share his suite over at the Aladdin. He took me to shows, introduced me to celebrities and embarrassed me by telling everybody what a great golfer he had with him. He kept telling me, "If I'd met you fifteen years ago, we would have won a ton of money, 'cause I had a lot of games." It was great fun being around him, but what I'll always remember most was his telling me that if I was up his way, not to check in anywhere else, just come and stay with him. When you're scuffling, that kind of thing makes you feel real good about yourself.

* * *

In the late '70s, Dickie Starnes and I played three or four times in an annual Captain's Choice tournament in Warsaw, Indiana. We only won it once, but we usually did all right up there and made some good contacts. One year Dickie got a call from a stockbroker he'd met in Warsaw who had some big games set up in Hawaii and wanted to fly him over.

Dickie played in Hawaii for the better part of a week, mostly against a Japanese businessman who couldn't do anything but lose. If the guy hit his ball in the water, Dickie would follow suit, sort of keep pace with the man's bad play. Dickie had a few other games, but when things thinned out a bit, he told his backers to fly me over there or he was leaving. They agreed to, since they really needed us on the high-stakes golf end. These guys were card sharps who would take care of the night action after we had carried the afternoons. Our deal was that we would keep sixty percent of our winnings after expenses. In the end, I think that they screwed us a bit, but we still took home about $25,000 for three weeks' work.

They put us up at the Waikiki Marina, which was gorgeous and all, but really, we didn't intend to stay as long as we did. It was a beautiful place, and I remember mist surrounding a mountain every morning, but it's not like we watched any hula dancers or ever went to the beach or anything. We were there on business.

One day we were playing against a couple of heavyset locals who we were kind of stringing along. We were trying not to get too far ahead on our $1,000 bet, so as not to scare anybody away. We had played them once before and they seemed all right—long hitters and lousy putters. Anyway, this particular round I was lining up a four footer on 18, when one of the opponents, who was some kind of island martial arts champ spoke up. "This is what I do to people who beat me out of money on the golf course," he said and proceeded to chomp a piece out of the side of a Titleist golf ball. He spit it out onto the green like a slice of sour apple. I missed the putt, which was probably the guy's intention, and we halved the match. Dickie took that piece of golf ball home and saved it for years.

Most of our other matches were less eventful, except for a Calcutta I played in on Maui. Calcutta tournaments are made up of four-man teams that each have an A, B, C, and D player. There's a lot of scamming and conning that goes into these tournaments, but all I can say here is they made all the A players into two handicaps, and I shot 65 for a net 63, which helped my team win the tournament. Someone got hot, and they weren't going to pay us. Then my B player, who turned out to be a Navy demolitions expert, threatened to blow up the damn clubhouse. We got paid.

Dickie and I mostly played a series of games against well-heeled businessmen, people who were in one way or another connected to our sponsors. It's a funny thing, but of all the millionaires I've run into on the golf course, most of them would rather win $500 on the links than make $20,000 in a day's business. In almost every case it's true, and you'll find this out when you get close to somebody and they open up over a few drinks. That's why even if they can afford to lose the money, they put extra pressure on themselves not to, since it means so much to them. You'd think that we're the ones that are supposed to be desperadoes, but in a golf match, it's often just the other way. And that just plays into my hands.

*   *   *

My favorite trip that Dickie and I took was a short one late one fall over to Tega Cay, a mountain course on the South Carolina border. We were down there playing with a fellow named John Jennings who was trying out a new set of irons. On the 9th hole, John hooked his tee shot out-of-bounds, then hit a second shot straight up the fairway. Walking up to his ball, he began snapping his clubs in half, one-by-one, throwing the pieces off the side of a hill that ran down into the woods. He went through every club except his wedge and putter. "I ain't crazy," he said. "I know I've still got a wedge shot to the green."

I started to go down after the broken clubs, figuring I would fix them up, put some new shafts on the heads, until John stopped me. "Leon," he said, yelling across the fairway, "if you retrieve so much as one of those clubs, I will attack you with this wedge." Well, he was pretty hot, and I certainly didn't need another set of clubs that bad, so I just let them be.

After the 9th hole, I mentioned something about how John might need some new sticks if we were going to continue. "We're not playing no more golf," he said, counting out the cash he owed. "But I do have my putter left, so how's about we have a puttin' contest?"

Dickie is an exceptional putter, I'm pretty good, and John is not what you'd call a "dead-eye." So there at about four in the afternoon we took him on. Before too long it got dark out and the lights came on outside the clubhouse. "Guys, let's go home," I said. It was getting cold, too. "I'm not gonna' stand out here on a putting green and freeze to death."

"We're not going home," said John. "We're going to keep puttin'. If you want to, you can get in the car and get warm for awhile, then come back and switch with Dickie."

Which is exactly what we did—we played him in shifts. We easily got him stuck over $2,000, since he was a lousy putter to begin with, plus one of us would come out warm from the car while John's hands were numbing up. Finally, it must have been around eight o'clock, his cash ran out and he called it quits. The only thing was, we'd had the car running off-and-on all that time, and I remembered that we'd been down pretty low on fuel when we first got there.

We ran out of gas a few miles down the road. Here we were with our winnings, in the middle of nowhere, in the pitch dark, ten to fifteen miles from the nearest open gas station. We started to walk a little ways and some horses in a nearby field neighed suddenly and scared the living shit out of us. Groping and stumbling, we made our way back to the car. We waited a long time for a car to come down the road. When it did, we flagged it down and asked some old-timer to do us a big favor. How much was it worth to us? he wanted to know, so we wound up giving him fifty for a lifty. Good thing we won.

Over the years, I have generally been up front about what I do, and how I do it. I always went full bore, even if it cost me, and it did, lots of times. My attitude was, who wants to play golf, how much? Let's go pardner, right now. And if I showed up in a strange place, or at a new golf course, I didn't try to go "undercover" or anything. It was more like, give me your best player, and let's get down. Disguising your game is just too stone cold; it's for people that want to stay on the run.

Now that's not to say I'm not looking to rob somebody out on the golf course. I am looking to do just that, by being the good player I represent myself to be, or used to be, anyway. However, there was one instance where I let good judgment and decency get away from me. There was some easy money involved, there was a money man, a set-up guy who arranged things, and I guess I just went along with the whole business. Call it greed and need.

It was in the early '70s when I met a top pool player and hustler named Marshall "The Squirrel" Carpenter. Squirrel was not too much of a golfer, but he had a group of guys down on a course in Mobile who liked to bet a ton of money. I first ran into Squirrel in a Charlotte poolroom where he'd beat me out of a few hundred dollars, not that big a deal since I was always live bait around that green felt. Squirrel knew about my golf reputation, so he took my number down, saying he had something going and that he'd call me.

He phoned a few weeks later and laid out a plan. We would go down to Mobile, and I would be introduced as an old friend of his, not using my real name. See, in gambling circles down South, word travels fast. While Leon Crump wasn't any household name, it probably would have rung a bell with guys playing high-dollar golf. So we changed my name to Larry something and I altered my swing and everything. The idea was to hit good shots—not all of the time—without ever looking like I had any kind of game. In fact, I think they set my handicap at 10, which, of course was nothing short of bold-faced larceny.

I had never done this before. I was playing with bad golfers who didn't stand a chance, and I felt guilty as hell. They were all great guys, and I would eventually one day find out that Squirrel had a beef with them, and this was his way of getting back. In a sense, I was just a pawn.

The first couple of days went by without a hitch. I did my best to hide my game and nobody suspected anything. They sure enough liked to gamble and our pockets were filling right up. I would duck-hook the ball, banana-slice it, miss greens on purpose, then get up-and-down as often as possible. The idea was to look lucky, although everybody who plays knows golf is not about luck. I never hit any three-, four-woods from the fairways for fear of hitting too long a ball. When I hit my irons, I used a short little swing, no follow through. I knew it was terrible for my tempo, so at night, I would sneak out to a driving range and hit balls with my natural swing—looking over my shoulder all the time to make sure no one saw me.

I think it was about the third or fourth round when I blew a shot that I was actually trying on and cursed myself in my own name, something like, "Goddammit Leon, what the hell are you doin'?" And I thought, Oh Lordy, now they know— it was like the whole world could hear it. In the meantime, they had started calling me "Punchy" for the way that I hit the ball. They would even give me advice about how I should follow through more after I hit the ball. They were always saying they couldn't believed I scored as well as I did.

Squirrel had also set me up as being from Tuscaloosa, which I even had trouble pronouncing. Then they'd ask me about this place or that restaurant, and I'd just do the best I could with it. I didn't feel right from the start, and I felt worse with my phony act once I got to know and like the guys I was playing against. Finally, in the clubhouse after they'd heard my real name on the course earlier, I fessed up.

"My name is Leon Crump," I told them, "I'm from Charlotte and I can play. I don't like this, and it wasn't my idea."

They listened to my confession, cussed Squirrel, and really just laughed the whole thing off. I didn't know what to expect, but since they took it so well, I hung around for another week playing to my normal speed. Nobody held anything against me, and I think I wound up about a $6,000, $7,000 winner. I even went back a few times over the years, playing as Leon Crump of course. But to these guys, my name never changed. To this day, at River Hills Golf Course in Mobile, I am known as Punchy.

13

Trying to Cut the Cut

When some people talk to me about golf, about the talent I've had and all the big games I've played, there's one subject that nearly always comes up—the pro tour. "Why is it, Leon"—they want to know—"that you never went out and made legitimate fame and fortune as a professional golfer?" With my game, they figure that I should have been out there taking down the purse money, waving to the crowds and making a household name of myself. Well, it's not all that simple.

To start with, as much as I've been on the road, I've always been a free agent. I could pick up any time and head back for home, which is where I really wanted to be anyway. I don't like staying in motels, I don't like hitting golf balls on the range, I don't like anybody telling me what time I've got to get up to get to the golf course, and I never cared for medal (stroke) play. Does that sound like the ideal profile of a professional golfer? I don't think so.

Besides, when I started playing golf for money in the early to mid-'50s, gambling often fetched better opportunities for top players than the pro tour did. Of course that would all change later on, but it really wasn't until the mid–'70s, or when I was almost 40 years old, that the tour started raining money. When I was first playing, you'd hear stories of Sam Snead and other pros skipping tournaments if they had a couple of pigeons on the line who potentially offered more than the next week's purse money, or next month's for that matter.

Myself, I didn't even need a pigeon to keep me afloat. Any old game would do—no matter how tooth-and-nail it was. Back then, gambling money went through our hands like water. You didn't need much to live, but there was always somebody around with a few thousand to shoot for, and as long as I was walking around with near that same size bankroll, I was fixed. The tour supported a few people, but only a very few. Even my mentor Clayton Heafner, who twice finished second in the U.S. Open, had to go looking for gambling games in addition to his club-pro income. It's not like today where the 150th ranked player in earnings pulls down two hundred thou a year.

Anyway, I have played some organized, professional golf over the years—enough to decide that I didn't like it. I reckon if I'd stuck to it a little more, I might have done better—but I never was big on the coulda-shoulda-woulda. If frogs had wings they wouldn't be frogs.

*   *   *

Some of the first professional golf I ever played was on the original "satellite" tours in the early '70s. That was down in Florida, on the old National Tournament Golf Association (NTGA) circuit before J. C. Goosie bought it out and turned it into the Space Coast Tour where a lot of today's top PGA players got their start. It was one tough scene.

There were some money games on the side, but never enough to really to suit me. I never could understand why more people didn't want to bet much in practice rounds, since the prize money didn't cut it. Winning outright might get you $2,000–$2,500, with second place worth maybe $1,500. Finishing in the top five hardly covered expenses. And these players were all hungry, which made the competition real rugged.

Once I was paired with a young pro from New England who was having himself a super day, just smoking the ball where he wanted it. I kept telling him "good shot" every time he stuck it up there, but I don't believe he said a word to me during the entire round. After we finished, he went to the tournament director, Tim O'Brien, who was a friend of mine, and told him he didn't want to be paired with me anymore. Tim asked him why, and the guy said to him, "He's too nice to play golf with. I can't play golf that way."

I laughed when I heard that, but it bothered me, because I hate to upset anyone on the course. So, I went up to talk to the guy, I told him that I was sorry, and that I hadn't meant to offend him in any way. He said, "Please don't take this wrong, but you kept telling me 'nice shot,' and I'm just not used to anybody doing that." We were never paired together again and it made a strong impression on me.

From then on, if I didn't know the tournament golfers I was playing with, I'd get up on the first tee, shake hands and ask, "Guys, when we play, does it bother you if I say 'good shot,' or would you rather I just keep my mouth shut?" I got some funny looks with that.

As far as I was concerned, there was no telling what was going to happen in these satellite tournaments. A few times, when I was too far back, I pulled out in the middle of a round to go and find me one of my good gambling games at Airco or any other nearby course. Why bang my head trying to get to eighth place for a bag of donuts when there were $500–$1,000 games around?

One of my son Bobby's fondest memories of those days was when he'd just graduated high school and was visiting me at a tournament down at Quail Hollow Golf Course in Zephyr Hills. He was himself a pretty good golfer by then and enjoyed spending the time with me and just being around the pro scene. I set him up the first day so he could hit practice balls all he wanted while I went out and played. He joined me on the back nine and watched me shoot 72, six strokes off the lead and a long way from pay dirt.

We got up the next morning and it was bright and sunny, about eighty degrees, what I considered a perfect day to lay back at the beach. All of a sudden, the golf didn't seem to matter so much, and I figured the same with Bobby, so I said, "Let's go hit the sand and forget about the tournament."

His jaw about dropped. "Dad," he said, "I don't want to go to the beach, I came here to watch you play golf. I want to watch you go out and try and win this thing."

Well, I figured if that's what my boy wants, let me go play. Since I was still far back from the lead, I suggested that Bobby go get something to eat and hit some balls while I played the front, then he could join me on the back nine. That gave me a little something to shoot for. At the turn, I spotted Bobby in the gallery, and when I gave him a hand-sign that I was four under par, he lit up. He followed me the rest of the way and having him out there just gave me a little extra juice. I shot 62 to take the lead, and it almost held up—almost. Eddie Pearce, who mostly played the PGA Tour, got up and down for birdie on 18, from a fairway trap, to nip me by a stroke. That day was special. Second place money wasn't worth all that much, but you can't put a price on some things.

Of course, I wouldn't likely have pulled up if I thought I had any chance to win. But on that particular day, when I felt like spending quality time with my son, it turned out that he made the right call for both of us by insisting that I play.

I had my share of top finishes down on those "mini-tours"—they tend to blur with the years—but I'll never forget the time that I almost quit on account of wildlife. I probably would have too, if Goosie hadn't been with me that day.

We were playing a swampy course near Orlando—I can't remember which, since so many cropped up around the same time. When I signed in at the pro shop, I saw that they had snake-bite kits for sale. That threw me just a bit, since I have a deathly fear of snakes and will not go near anyplace where I think they might be lurking. Down South, that's a real golfing handicap, since you've got snakes mostly everywhere there's golf courses. In the back of my mind, I'm playing "no-hunt" golf, meaning that I will take a penalty stroke rather than look for a ball in any kind of swampy area.

Late in the tournament, I'm playing with Goosie, in contention, and we see a big old copperhead lying across the cart path. My ball is very close, lying up nice, but near some palmettos where the snake had just come out of.

"I ain't goin' near that thing," I told Goosie, and I waited for it to move. It just sat there, or lay there rather, until

Goosie threw a stick at it. That's when it got up straight, coiled up like it wanted to strike. Whoa, now! I waited some more—I was about frozen in my tracks—and Goosie said something about how we had to get going, we were holding up play. "Penalize my ass," I told him.

Finally, the snake moved away; I went and hit my ball, fast. I hit nothing higher than four- or five-irons off the tee the rest of the day and fell down off the leader board. I didn't care; I wanted to make sure that I left myself no chance to be anywhere but the middle of the fairway. I promise you, snakes will get to my nervous system, and people I play with regularly know that. Back at Eastwood, Dickie Starnes about gave me a heart attack once when he snuck a rubber snake under my towel in the golf cart.

Another memory that haunts me from around that period was a rules violation by another player down at Magnolia, a beautiful course in the Disney complex. If I had called it the way I should have, I would have won the damn golf tournament.

The situation involved a pro golfer who's now a well-known name on the Pro Tour. He was a kid with a lot of talent then, hadn't played much tournament golf, and I was trying to help him. Early in that final round, he was marking his ball improperly on the green with a tee. I didn't call it, I just told him he had better start using a coin, which he did.

But the killer was at the 17th hole, when we were tied for the tournament lead. He snap-hooked his drive into a lateral water hazard, took his penalty and made what appeared to be an improper drop. If he was judging where his ball first crossed the hazard line, he placed himself way too far up (toward the green) for his third shot. Well, it's a judgment call, but I, and the others in our group, let it go when we shouldn't have. There's an obligation to call it, because if you don't, you're doing everybody else in the tournament an injustice. I guess where I was coming from, I was just used to letting things like that slide.

Anyway, he knocked it up on the green and made his putt to tie me with a 4. We tied the next and final hole, and he beat me on the 1st hole in a sudden death playoff. So you let people do stuff sometimes they shouldn't, and it'll get you, one way or another. He wound up being a real good player, but who knows, that win might have put him over the hump. The kicker is, I've seen that boy around a few times since, and he acts like he don't even know me.

One of the major reasons I never did so well in tournament golf was that my personality wasn't suited to stroke or medal play. Like the Kevin Costner character in the movie *Tin Cup*—more on that a little later—I usually went straight for the flag, for better or for worse. Tour players play conservative golf—not all of the time, but at least when they have to. Laying up, playing safe, taking the fat part of the green, lagging putts, splittin' the fairway with three woods—all the things you need to do to control your overall score—were just never part of my game, which is a full-bore, match play game. Match play is a totally different animal, totally different mental approach.

In match play, you play the player, not the course. Even when you do alter strategy on some shots because of the course—what they generally call "course management"—it's still because of your opponent and how he faces the situa-

143

tion. I call it match play-course management. For instance, say I'm looking at a narrow fairway on a par 4 surrounded by woods, and I'm in a close match. Because I'm already long off the tee, I might play a long-iron safe shot and let the other guy try and make a run at it with his driver. The idea is to try to force him to make the mistake. Now if a guy's a little longer and gonna go shoot for the pin, I won't hesitate to hit the driver.

There are some people who cannot stand to have you drive the ball past them. For some reason—and I think there's usually a lot of ego involved—it really upsets them, and they'll be coming off their heels, swingin' out of their boots to catch up. When I play a guy like that, I won't hold anything back, just make sure I'm out there so far enough that I can almost make him overswing. You just have to play each individual.

Sure, there's still your usual course management. You have to know where your trouble's at and where you don't want the ball to go, regardless of what club you hit. Of course, if a guy hits a real bad shot and winds up in the slammer, you've got to play as safely as you know how for that hole—you're a fool not to. You have to play an individual according to the way he plays, think in terms of how the game will go based on the way he's going to play. It's not like tournament golf—trying to make sure you make a par here, a par there, and then maybe you might birdie this or that hole.

In match play, there are certain times when you have to go out and overpower your opponent; if you lay back too much, then first thing you know, you're down and he's got you. Even if I only need par, I might try extra hard to birdie the par 5s every time out. I want my opponent to feel that he needs an eagle to win.

My old friend Charley Miller likes to remind me that I once told him I'd love to play Jack Nicklaus one round for a $1,000,000. I can't remember saying it, but I probably did, since I certainly used to think along those lines. I'd sure like to have the $1,000,000 to play him, but I don't think I'd risk it all today, even if I hit the lottery. What I really meant back then was that I wanted to play a great player like Nicklaus, match play where we'd have equal pressure on us. Problem is, today I'd need to put up an oil company to get near stakes that'd make him quiver.

For somebody who doesn't cotton to medal play, trying to qualify for a PGA Tour exemption (the right to play PGA tournaments) is strong medicine. I did buck it a few times at the Qualifying School, and I did come close, but I never made it. Probably my most frustrating try was in Tuscon in 1970.

They call it a "school," but it's actually a grueling tournament where several hundred players slug it out over four days for ten or twelve spots. (Today they play a total of five rounds.) The school part of it I guess is from the lectures and the test they give you on rules and such. I didn't have any problem with knowing the rules, but that didn't keep me from a real costly bonehead move on my final round in the desert.

My caddy and I were up at the putting green before the round, trying to decide on what clubs to carry. Of course the rules of golf only allow you fourteen, which makes for a hard choice sometimes on what to leave behind. In this case it was between a one-iron and a five-wood. I decided to go with the five, and gave the caddie my car keys and told him to go put the one-iron in the trunk.

I was in pretty good shape all the way and was looking solid to earn a spot coming down the final nine. On the 17th hole, I had a long shot to an elevated green and asked my caddie for the five-wood. He said no, take a two-iron, which surprised me, since we'd so far agreed on just about every club choice all week. He kept insisting on the two, until finally I just went to grab the five for myself.

Right away, I saw why we had a problem. The one-iron was stuck up in there, under the five's head cover. He had forgotten to get rid of the extra club and was trying to hide it. I had been carrying fifteen sticks for sixteen holes. He apologized and said he realized his mistake after we started and was just trying to get back to the clubhouse without me realizing what had happened.

"Jeez, man," I said to him. "Why didn't you throw it in a lake or something, if you didn't want me knowing it?"

He knew what I had to do once I saw it, and I did too. The penalty for carrying too many clubs back then was four strokes. I called it on myself and wound up two shots off what I needed to qualify. The caddie looked like he wanted to kill himself right there, but hell, it was just as much my fault for not double-checking my bag before I started. For a long time after that, I was counting clubs trying to get to sleep nights.

The next year, I tried to qualify at Tanglewood, a course I knew fairly well, right here in North Carolina. I played three pretty good rounds, but then the last day I shot 72 and missed getting a spot by one stroke. I was playing with long-time top pro Lanny Wadkins, and he did make it in his first try, shooting 62 on the final round. I think Lanny kind of rocked me to sleep that day, as good as he was playing. See, my problem was instead of taking on the course, I was hung up in a match play mind-set. Subconsciously, I was playing Lanny instead of the rest of the field and it cost me.

Former major-league ball player Hawk Harrelson was also paired with us that day. He didn't make it and neither did the oddball who was our fourth man. I can't recall his name, but I will never forget the guy hitting the ball dead perfect down the middle, then go walking through the deep woods every time to come back up to his ball. He did this a number of times; instead of joining us up the fairway, he'd be thrashing around in the weeds, taking a round-about route to his ball. He had us all wondering what he was up to, but we never found out what that was about. Maybe he was looking for golf balls.

I had a couple of other tries to qualify for the Senior Tour and came up empty, but it was always real close. People always talk about the pressure and how it's like Elvis (now or never), and it may be for some, but I just never looked at it that way. I knew that when I left the qualifier, I'd always go back to a game somewhere. I was a match-play player and I'd go back to that. The others would mostly go back to their jobs, which they of course didn't want to do. With such a slim chance to begin with, they had everything to lose. Now that's what I call pressure.

Probably the biggest highlight of my humble pro career was playing the U.S. Open, at Hazeltine, up in Minneapolis, in 1970. That was the year the runner-up, Dave Hill, made headlines by calling the course a "cow patch" and saying they ought to replant it in clover. Hell, where I was coming from, that track seemed about manicured. As a matter of fact I thought it was in damn good shape. The weather was pretty bad though, so bad we didn't get but one practice round in. And the greens were about as tough as any I've ever played. It wasn't so much their speed, which was plenty slick, as it was their shape and contours. Some of 'em were about sloped like an old car hood—hit too short and you'd roll back down; hit too long and you'd roll off the other way.

I had made it to that Open by qualifying beforehand in a regional tournament at the Charlotte Country Club. There was a tie with five players for the last four playoff spots and we went into sudden-death, knowing that one of us wouldn't make it—kind of like Russian Roulette. Bob Charles was one of the five, and he was begging the USGA people down there to let us all in, but they wouldn't go for it. For one time, I decided to play baby-safe as I knew how, and sure enough, one of the others made bogey and didn't get to go.

I was tickled when a couple of my Eastwood pals, Charlie Miller and Whitey Moses, took their wives and traveled up to Hazeltine to "sweat" me in the big time. Some local sports-writers had already played me up in the news—"CHAR-LOTTE HUSTLER PLAYS OPEN" and all that sort of stuff—and now I felt like I had my own private gallery. I knew my pals were making bets all over the place, me against differ-ent golfers, head up, and of course it didn't bother me at all. Charley bet Jim Dent's manager a substantial amount on opening day and had to go chase him down in the parking lot afterwards to get paid. These are things you'll never see on TV.

Now about that movie *Tin Cup*, specifically the scene

where Kevin Costner gets to the Open and starts shanking balls on the practice range like a rank amateur. I don't know where they got the idea for that, but I swear that very same thing happened to me right up there at the main event. The moment I got up to the practice tee, I began feeling very out of place. There was Nicklaus, Palmer, Player, all the big names, casually chatting between hits like they didn't have a care in the world.

I took, I think, an eight-iron just to loosen up with, and my very first hit went squirtin' off sideways, in full of view of a grandstand full of spectators. I took a few more swings and got the very same result. I couldn't believe it, and I couldn't really understand it either—I had suddenly come down with the worst case of shanks I'd ever had. (The "shanks"—clunking the ball off to the right—defy understanding; the best thing anybody can do is clear your mind and get back to basics.)

Whatever it was, I had to get the hell out of there. I couldn't let anybody, pros or spectators, see me in that condition. It was brutal, but I left the grounds and went and found me a public driving range. Away from the center stage, I got a little more comfortable, and it didn't take me long to get the rock to behave itself.

The next day, in between rainstorms, I had shook off the shanks and managed to go out and play some damned decent golf. I was on the leaderboard for a couple of blinks, which about scared me half-to-death, but I came in with a 74, which in those conditions, wasn't half bad. I think I birdied three out of the first five holes, while the wind was howlin' so bad, it brought down the hospitality tents. The next day some more rain came, and I shot 75 and made the cut.

It'd be nice to say that I made a run at it, but over the final two rounds, I just kind of fell out of sight the way ninety-five percent of all pro golfers do every weekend. That's the cold-blooded reality of tournament golf—can't but one man win and a handful of others contend. At least I didn't shoot as high as 80, and there were plenty of those out there. But whether or not anybody knew who I was, I certainly gave the folks up at the 17th hole something to take back home on my final round.

The hole is a short-and-narrow par 4 that had me hitting with a two- or three-iron off the tee. On my last go-round, I had about 160 yards to the hole, when I swung me a pluperfect, sweet little ole' eight-iron that shot out at the pin like a heat-seekin' missile. It landed about twenty feet past the flag, hit reverse, and spun back to the cup like a yo-yo. I couldn't really see it, but I knew it had a chance, and when the people around the green started raising tee-total hell, I realized I'd knocked it in for eagle. At that point, it wasn't much more than whipped cream on shit, but it was still a nice way to finish up.

Over the years—the past three decades, anyway—I have played a number of well-known professional golfers. Maybe not all are household names, but they've all made noise at one time or another on the PGA Tour. I've had my share of gambling games, with some, not all, of these guys and for the most part, it was just like dukin' it out with anybody else back home. I'm never one to be affected or all that impressed by players with fancy credentials, because I do know one thing—name won't get it in the hole.

Lon Hinkle, Larry Mowrie, Leonard Thompson, and Randy Glover, are just a few of the many names that jump back at me from the past. Just about anytime I'm watching Seniors golf on TV, I'll hear names—say, Colbert, Ziegler, Jacobs, Stroble, whoever—that I hooked up against at one time or another. Down in Tampa when I was fussin' with the mini-tour, I played a lot of these guys fifty, hundred dollar games—good tough games, competitive games where nobody gets waxed. Of course I always tried to jack it up, work in a higher bet to get them out of their comfort zone, but generally it was hundred-dollar stuff.

Frank Beard, who's now an announcer for ESPN, gave me some pretty good tussles, first down in Ocala, Florida, then later when he used to come up to Charlotte for the Kemper Open. He was a classy player, a gentleman with a dry sense of humor and a ton of gamble in him. The last time we tangled, Dickie Starnes and I beat him and Jimmy Yancey out of over $5,000 (we played Frank different combinations of partners). When it was over, we all shook hands, and I remember Frank saying "Boys, I'm not gonna let you rob my friends anymore. We can't win." But Frank was a great gin player, and we gave a substantial part of that money back when he skunked us at cards that night.

Down at Lone Palm, in Lakeland, I got very lucky partnering up with Andy Bean right after he'd come out of college. Nobody really knew his speed yet, but he just owned the course there the way he played, and we did very well. Lanny Wadkins and Ray Floyd are two names that come up when people talk about betting games on the tour. Most of this stuff is exaggerated, but I have played Wadkins, nothing too big, and as far as Floyd, well, some people in Vegas were once trying to put together a $50,000 match between me and him, but it never came off. Of course I was ready and willing, but I think he had other commitments or they couldn't reach him, I'm not sure.

On two separate occasions, I played some pretty hefty-sized matches with big-named golfers who, when contacted recently, did not want their names used in this book. I will respect their wishes, even if in my mind there was nothing wrong or harmful about what happened—unless if you consider the fact that they lost their money to me on the golf course (I won't even say where we played). It's funny when you think about it. Real gamblers don't mind at all bringin' up their major losses—most of 'em even brag about it. But I guess when somebody's made it to a certain point in their career, they don't want to be reminded about once getting hammered by a scuffler like myself.

On the subject of famous names, people ask me a lot about Michael Jordan, since it came out that he played some high-dollar golf around Charlotte. I never played with him and never even met him, although I do know most of the people who supposedly won all that money from him. There were times when there was talk of us playing, but nobody called me and I just stayed away from it, didn't feel like pushing myself in. Michael's probably heard of me from around the Charlotte area, and I'm 100 percent sure that without all the negative publicity about his golf games, we probably would have played a bunch by now.

But what I don't understand is, here's a man who's made all the money that anybody could ever need, yet the people in his business won't let him do what he wants to do with it. If he wants to go blow some money on the golf course, that's his right. Hell, he probably makes more just in interest during a round of golf, than he could possibly lose. Why don't they leave him alone and let him do what he wants to with his money? To him, betting a golf game is a way to relax away from basketball, so in a sense, they're not letting him enjoy his life. I could understand maybe if he was hanging with bookies and betting NBA games, but we're talking about gambling at a game of skill and choosing the company you wish. Michael's money looks nice from here, but if it ever got to the point where I couldn't bet, I wouldn't want to be that famous.

Just a few more thoughts on the pro tour. Even if I never made it to the big show, I'd be lying if I said it wasn't on my mind at different times. Everybody thinks about it. Some people want it a lot more than others. Anybody that's good enough that wants to give it a shot—it's out there. They're giving away big money. If you're lucky enough to get there—and believe me you got to have some luck—it's a glamorous life, I'm sure.

But for all the killer instinct I used to have on the golf course, I suffered a little bit in the ambition department. I like sleeping in my own bed, and not living out of a suitcase—which of course I've had to do from time to time. I've been really lucky in that I've always made a good living playing golf around home, or within a short drive, anyway. I will say it's damn near impossible to make the tour if you don't really want to.

You've probably heard Lee Trevino's old line about pressure's when you're playing a match for five dollars and you only have three in your pocket. In my case, you can multiply that a few times. What he was really talking about was that he didn't really feel any pressure on tour, playing for money he can't lose out of his own pocket; I feel exactly the same way about the pro game.

There is one golf tournament that any good golfer in his right mind would like to be in on and that's the Skins Game. I see that event as a duck shoot for dough. Talk about handing out free money—that one is a freewheeler. If you can't lose nothing and it costs nothing to play, how could there be any pressure? I suppose there's pressure in trying to be the top money winner in the two-day event, but I think it would be real relaxing to play in.

I have the utmost respect for PGA Tour players; I think it's great they're playing for the money they are when they're putting up so little. They're very dedicated, and they've all worked hard on their games to get where they're at. I'm sure it is a grind and all. But when you talk about lining up a putt that's worth $5,000, it's a lot harder to make that putt, when you know missing it is going to cost you $5,000. Take it from me, I've been there a few times.

14

Cheating

"Golf is the hardest game in the world to play and the easiest to cheat at," pro golfer Dave Hill once said. It's also the only sport played on the honor system, which has been known to cause a few problems in some gambling games. There may be honor among thieves, but not a whole lot of it among golfing thieves. I can attest to that from personal experience.

The white rock is just too damn small. Too many things can happen to it, things that are usually in direct violation of the USGA Rules of Golf. When it comes to plain old bald-ass cheating, I have seen just about every variety. I have seen balls thrown from a sand trap; I have seen balls somehow come flying out from deep woods, from places where you need a machete just to get into, where you couldn't possibly get a full swing with a golf club; I have seen people with an amazing knack for "finding" lost balls; I have seen balls lying out in the middle of a fairway mysteriously disappear; I have seen every kind of bad lie improved; I have seen golf balls kicked around, and I've seen them switched; and as far as totaling up strokes, I have seen every kind of creative accounting there is.

Really, everybody'd be a whole hell of a lot better off if the rules of golf could simply be reduced to one: do not touch your ball from the time you tee it up, until the time you take it out of the cup on the green. The USGA doesn't have anything in their book about actual "cheating." They're more polite about it and think more in terms of obeying rules. Many of the rules of golf get broken out of pure ignorance, and if you're playing a match with the same set of "wrong" rules, well, what's good for the goose is good for the gander. It all evens out. But a lot of golfers know the rules and will go out of their way to avoid them. To these guys, it ain't cheating if you don't get caught.

Much of the cheating you can spot takes place on the green and has to do with marking the ball. The most obvious ploy is when a player tries to gain a couple of extra inches by moving his ball too far in front of the coin or marker he laid down. The nerve of some of these people is something else, depending on how blatant the violation is. Do they think that you're not going to notice what they're doing? Hell, once you get to the green, all eyes are on a putter's every move. Cheaters tend to think the world is made of suckers.

Personally, I don't mind to see guys fudging a bit on the green, because that's just another sign of weakness. Those couple of inches aren't going to help that much if the guy's got the yips; in fact, it's usually an indication that he's fixing to miss his putt. What is amazing to me is how many people mark improperly. People will mark to the side of where their ball actually lies so's to avoid the little hole from a golf shoe spike mark, or to stay clear of a dollar spot or indentation, whatever. Hey, where you wind up is all part of golf—rub of the green, I believe they call it. Also, how about the guys that lay a coin *in front of* their ball, then move the ball, then go put the ball back down *in front* of the coin—they've just gained a couple of ball widths closer to the hole with that fraud. I actually saw a guy do that in a tournament. It's tough to call somebody on something like that; if they were nervy enough to do it in the first place, they'll damn sure deny it when you accuse them.

The hardest thing I ever ran into was down in Ocala, Florida, with a couple of guys I was playing individually, two matches at the same time. We had been playing over a couple of days and even though they weren't playing so hot, I couldn't get a leg up. We were riding in separate carts and they were usually off on the other side of the fairway, green, whatever. After a couple of rounds, it dawned on me that on the greens, they were taking what seemed like shorter putts than what I expected each time they marked their ball. In other words, I would watch them hit their shot—say on a par 3—watch it land and roll, and figure in my mind, oh well, that's about a twenty-foot putt. Then they'd get up there, mark their ball, and I'd see where they actually had a 13- or 14-footer. I'd just figure, well, I guess he's closer than I first thought he was.

Now this happened on a few more holes, and then the alarm went off. Hey, that's three, four times I thought they had twice as much real estate on a putt than they actually did—what's up here? I happened to get up a little closer, paid a little more attention and, lordy, I caught on. When I realized what they were up to, I about jumped out of my Footjoys.

One of these snakes had him a little pin magnet set into the bottom of his putter blade. He had a marker or coin that the magnet could pick up, and when he was patting down his line, he would actually lift up the marker and place it back down closer to the hole, or close enough so's to have a better chance of holing out. Now you take five, six feet off a half-dozen medium range putts enough times over a few rounds and you can turn a close match into an out-and-out heist.

When I confirmed it by grabbing the man's putter and taking a close look at his set-up, I said, "Fellas, we got trouble here." The magnet man tried to act like he didn't know what the hell I was talking about, said that the magnet was "just a metallic insert to add weight" to his putter. The other guy got all huffy and quit, accused me of being paranoid and called all the bets off.

Now the funny thing is, I kept playing with the magnet man, even if he had tried to cheat me. I felt no need to get righteous and quit. Don't get angry, I told myself, just get the money—it's still there. I told him that if we were to continue he, would have to mark with a plastic mark I gave him, and he said all right—just about flat-out admitting he'd cheated. I watched him like a hawk the rest of the way, but I think his conscience must have gotten to him, because I don't think he won another hole that day.

"A little dab'll do you," that's what the old ad used to say. When applied properly to the face of the golf club, just a smidgeon of Chapstick, K Y jelly, Vaseline, slippery elm, or any other similar kind of grease, will make the golf ball fly straight and long as a Texas highway. Grease cuts down on your sidespin, making it a lot harder to hit those nasty ole' hooks and slices. And with your iron's grooves filled, the ball will fly another ten, twenty yards farther, too. Of course, greasing your clubheads is about as illegal as it gets in golf, but that never held some people back in my neck of the woods.

The first time I ever caught onto it was in the late '50s when Stuart Bragg first came around Eastwood. Like any wise old hustler, the man had a full bag of tricks. One summer day, we were out playing in what must have been about ninety-five degrees in the shade, and Bragg, who was usually pretty wild out of the tee box, was hittin' the pill straight down the middle. We had never seen him do that. On the back nine, I happened to notice that the back of his shirt was messed up with something oily. There was a trail of whatever it was running down from behind his ear.

I mentioned something about the mess he had on his shirt, but he didn't really pay me any mind, just kind of shied away from me. One of the other guys we were playing with heard me, came over to have a look and laughed. He told me Bragg was using grease, that people would sometimes sneak a little splotch of it behind their ear and go to it when they needed it. Well, nobody made too big a deal of it—they just told Bragg to wipe off his clubs (and his ear, too), that's all. He did, and he went back to hooking the ball, and we finished the round. I still didn't know exactly what the hell was goin' on.

Next day, I tried it out myself, and I was surprised at the results. When I used the driver, I think the way I swung so hard must have hampered the grease effect. With the woods, the ball stuck to the clubface too much and probably cost me distance. But when I tried a greased-up five-iron, I could practically turn the club into a driver—the ball fired off of that sucker like it was a launched rocket.

I never really played the stuff much, even though some guys would out-and-out insist on it as a handicapping tool. "We're playin' grease today, goddamit," they'd say.

"Hell no, we ain't," somebody else was sure to answer.

Problem is, grease doesn't help the scratch player so much as it does help an 80-shooter. The way you can tell if a player's using it, other than if it's running down his shirt, is the ball sort of flutters in mid-flight. It'll get about 75, 100 yards out then kind of wobble, like a knuckle ball. Unless you know what you're looking for, it's tough to really spot it.

Whitey Moses, an old buddy of mine, had an excellent short game and would often insist on playing grease, when we'd let him. One particular day, we were playing with Dave Sorensen and we had specifically agreed on no grease. We got up on the 16th tee, Dave hit his ball, and I could see it wiggle before it straightened out. "Dave," I said, "we're playing no grease, buddy. You got grease on that club." See, I knew he was subject to sticking it up on us, and when I saw that baby shake and shimmy, I knew he had done just that. It pissed me off a little since we had decided against it beforehand.

"Well, you caught me," was all Dave said.

I went and grabbed the driver out of his hand and rubbed all the grease off into the dirt of the cart path. "Hey Dave," Whitey laughed. "You made Leon's shit hot."

Dave just laughed back. "I'd rather his shit be hot than mine."

There have been a lot of larcenous s.o.b.'s in my past, but one of my old regular opponents goes right to the top of the list. The strange thing about this guy was, he could get just as much satisfaction out of cheating somebody as he would beating them on the square. Sometimes he'd say, "Well if you catch me cheatin', just call the hole right there." Like what the hell else were we going to do, let him cheat? The man could flat out stick it; let him mess with the rules on top of that, and you'd wind up one broke puppy dog.

The hell of it is, having to concentrate on anything other than your golf game will help you lose—especially if you've got to be worried about what somebody else may or may not be doing. The man knew that and worked it to the max. "Better watch me," he'd tell you, and it was true.

One time the guy—call him Dick, since I don't need him suing my ass—was betting Catfish some way or another, and Catfish was helping Dick look for a ball. Now in most cases, players aren't in too much of a hurry to join the search party since a lost ball usually means a lost hole. But in Dick's case, you just didn't want to leave him off alone. After a bit, Catfish saw Dick drop a ball through a hole in his back pocket, down his pant leg. The ball hit the back of his golf shoe and ran about ten yards down the fairway. It had hardly stopped rolling when Dick called out, "Oh, there it is."

"Bullshit!" Catfish exploded. "I just saw you drop another ball."

Leave it to Dick to try and come out of it. "If I did that," he said, "and I'm not saying I did, you couldn't possibly have seen me. I was watching you, and you were looking the other way."

One time a bunch of us were out playing at Cedarwood, and while we were waiting to hit on one tee, Charlie Miller started bouncing a ball off his wedge. He wasn't all that good at it, and somebody mentioned Zan Long, who we all knew as the best ball-bouncer who ever lived. One thing led to another and it wound up where Dick was going to bet a $1,000 that Zan, whom he'd never seen, couldn't bounce it 500 times without missing.

We all jumped on it, since we knew Zan could probably walk an entire nine holes through a rainstorm and keep bouncing the ball without missing. He was amazing; he could bounce it high, kill it on the club, bounce it low and fast—anyway he wanted, for as long as he wanted. About the only way he would ever screw up was if somebody knocked him down. We called up Zan, got him over there, and offered him a piece of the bet, which he accepted. That made us feel better, since you never know—maybe he hadn't practiced for a while or had a sore wrist.

He started up at a pretty good pace—pop, pop, pop, pop, pop, pop—and Dick was doing the counting. Now of course, Dick had to work it his way, which he did by making just one count to Zan's every two bounces. Zan didn't care, he kept bouncing along like he was on his way to 10,000. When Zan got over 400, Dick slowed the count down even more as Zan neared the finish line. But he got there no sweat and kept on bouncing till we told him to quit. You'd have thought Dick would've been upset about losing the money, but he wasn't. The way he saw it, he felt like a winner since he'd slow-counted Zan and made him bounce 600, 700 times more than what the bet called for. Win or lose, cheating and getting over on people was sometimes victory enough for Dick. Strange man.

People don't pay nearly enough attention to what brand and number ball a player's using. In some games, not knowing that can be a head start for handing the money over. One time, I played two guys individually (again, separate matches), betting one player a $200 nassau and the other $600. I never thought about it until one of the eyeballers clued me in later, but the $600 bettor often had the best drive and usually wound up closest to the pin—whether he actually was or not. They were exchanging each other's balls all day and I was blind to it. They wouldn't do it if I was right there or if there was a huge difference in distance, but if it meant a good lie or a straighter putt, if I wasn't paying attention, they would run with it.

The boldest move I ever heard of was one time at Eastwood, late one day when it was getting dark. On the par-3 9th, one of the players left his ball in the hole, then challenged his opponent to playing the last four holes again. They rode out there, started playing and by the time they got to the 9th all even, you needed a flashlight to find the tee. When it was his turn to hit, the boy who left his ball in the cup took out a two-iron, which the other guy couldn't see, and nailed it about a hundred yards past the green. Just after he hit it, he yelled something like, "Oh baby—get in the hole!" like he'd just made a perfect shot. They went up to the green, and of course, the guy found his ball a "hole in one."

There was a crazy foursome out at Eastwood who played the cheatingest damn game you'd ever want to see. The whole point of their game was to cheat, if you could, without getting caught. If you got caught, you would just lose the hole. Afterwards, over drinks, you couldn't shut 'em up when it came to bragging about this hole or that hole, when they did this or that, and nobody caught them.

A lot of times, people play "inside the leather" on a putt. This is a gimme, meaning: you put the putter in the cup and lay it down alongside your ball. If it's inside the grip, the putt is good. One day, one of these thieves played an entire round with his grip cut back some three, four inches. I don't know that it made that big a difference, but he sure was quick to show it off afterwards. From that time on, they all made a big production of making sure everybody's grip length was equal before they started play.

The way these guys played, you could call somebody on cheating, but you had to actually catch him, not guess, otherwise, the penalty was on you. This led to some interesting arguments. One time, two of these guys were haggling over whether or not one of them could have seen the other move his ball in the rough, since the cart was supposedly in the way. They went back to the spot and set it up again, and they switched places so that the cheater could verify that the opponent had actually had a clear sight line. Then the cheater admitted that the caller was right, could have seen him, and he went ahead and gave him the hole.

My personal favorite is a variation on a story that's as old as the hills. In this case, these players were back in the clubhouse talking about all the dirt they'd done each other during the round. "Hey," said one to another. "Remember that shot on 12, where I was having trouble finding my ball? Well I just dropped me another ball."

"You did?" said one of the others. "This wouldn't be your original ball, would it?" he asked, pulling the man's Titleist that he, himself, had lifted back at the hole.

I don't know how these guys could look at themselves in the mirror every morning, but at least they were all up front about it, unlike another Eastwood foursome. In that game, the players were so paranoid about anybody cheating, they had a rule that if your hands ever went below your knees, it was a one-stroke penalty.

Whew! Trying to play golf and cope with all that would make my head spin.

15

Cheap Advice

Golf lessons have always been kind of alien to me. I understand the need for them and how people come to rely on them, but for me, the best parts of the golf swing come from the do-it-yourself school. By that I mean watching other golfers and learning from them what to do and what not to do, what works and what doesn't, and what to take for yourself personally. Doesn't matter whether you're talking grip, address, swing plane, whatever—it's all adjustable. Same thing applies with the mental aspects of the game. It was only after too many years as a hothead that I learned about composure and keepin' your cool, which seems to work a little better with golf. Also, with gambling and making games—over time you tend to make fewer mistakes, keep from jumping into the same traps, especially when you see them come around again.

When I began to play, really I just swung at the ball and didn't think too much about anything—kind of carved my game out of raw muscle. It was later on that I fine-tuned it, but not all that much. I guess the dumber you are, the easier golf gets. Too much going on upstairs will ruin the best of swings—guaranteed. I've seen it happen all too often.

To my mind, the late, great teacher Harvey Penick said it all when he told people just to "take dead aim." That's pretty much the extent of the swing thought I would like to have. It may sound over-simplified when you're dealing with something as seemingly complex as the golf swing, but that's just it—you want to keep it simple.

So what I'm going to lay out here are some simple thoughts about a complicated game. Of course everybody's different, and I wouldn't pretend to be able to customize anybody's game. But what I believe I can offer are some basic down-home approaches to help people get their rounds in and maybe stop the bleeding. It's been my experience that on every level of play, there are consistent winners and consistent losers. If you've been victimized a little more than you'd like in your regular games, it's never too soon to put a stopper on it.

FINISH HIGH. That right there was the first bit of self-correction I ever used when my shots started going off line—this was once I realized that my game was not bulletproof, that I wasn't going to automatically knock it straight forever. When you make the right finish in your swing, the chances of your staying on line are greatly increased. The key is the back of the left hand. Let the back of your left hand sweep through your finish toward the target and try and finish high. When you watch a good player, check out the end of his swing. Chances are he's got the back of his left hand moving through on target. Sometimes just focusing on that little part, the end of the swing, will pull together all the business that goes on before it. In a nutshell, you want to complete the swing.

PRACTICE WITH ONE CLUB. I was never one to go bang balls on the range; I just never had the patience for it. But I do believe you've got to do something when your game starts tailing off—regardless where it's tailing off from. When the wheels fall off too many times, when I'm having trouble getting the ball to go where I want it, what I like to do is go out on the course with only one club and play an entire round that way (usually by myself, unless I can get a game). I prefer a five-iron, but you can take anything from a two-iron to a wedge, it doesn't really matter. Without even thinking about it, you'll become more focused on your tempo and your feel.

Practicing with one club will get you more focused on distances and what you have to do with your swing and your hands to overcome the shot, whether it's a drive, a sand blast (open up the blade if you've got, say, a four-iron), a putt (chip it or blade it). Then of course, when you tackle the game with your full set of sticks, you're more in tune with each club and how it was designed to suit every type of shot. Try it out sometime, and you'll also be surprised with how well you can do with a single club. Remember, playing one club is easier on a flat course; best to try this where the ball will run.

PRACTICE PUTTING WITH A WEDGE. When you think about it, regulation putting is thirty-six shots per round, or half of par—that's the way the game is set up. An average of close to two of your shots on every hole will be putts, so it's without doubt the most important part of scoring. Yet it never ceases to amaze me how many golfers come up with something like, "Man, if I could putt, I'd be dangerous." Many of those very same guys are the least likely to go practice their putting. And that's another thing that I've found about a lot of average players—they tend to practice the better, but never the worse, parts of their game.

The dreaded yips will hit everybody at one time or another, and the only thing you can do to correct them is go back to basics. The reason for missing two-to-four-foot "knee-knockers" are many. Picking the putter up, being jerky, peeking at the hole too soon, and flopping the wrist are just a few examples. To get straightened out, what I like to do is take a wedge out to the practice green and use it to putt with for about a half-hour. What this does is force me to be as still as possible, in order to catch the ball with the edge of the blade just right to get it rolling center-cup. The best putting golfers you will ever see are as still as wooden Indians when they stroke it (Ben Crenshaw is a prime example).

A couple of other strategical putting tips: (1) Know your elevation on longer putts. Too may people concern themselves too much with which way the ball will "break" instead of what the speed is. They tend to overlook the up or downhill factor to any putt unless it's really extreme or obvious. (2) Try and keep the ball below the hole on the last four holes. Not that you can place the ball exactly where you want it, but believe me, you want to stay away from leaving yourself short downhill putts when there's money on the line. Those are visits to the throw-up zone.

JUDGE SHORT DISTANCE BY FEEL. When I was growing up, we didn't have 150- or 100-yard markers. We knew pretty much what distance required what club, and we managed to play pretty sporty that way. When they're inside 100 yards, people today waste entirely too much time pacing off exact yardage, when they don't have that much of a repeating swing to benefit by it anyway. There are just not that many golfers with the ability to hit, say, eighty-four yards on the nose, as opposed to eighty-six. What this does, besides slow down play, is make people way too reliant on information that's going to vary anyway with green conditions, wind conditions, and the obvious fact that they don't likely put the same swing on it every time. Go on and take your wedge out, take a hard look at the pin, and just put the swing on it—however long and hard, or short and easy you feel is best.

Another thing: getting spin on the ball may look nice on TV, but it's of no real use to most golfers. You might benefit from that shot when you've got a downhill slope to a pin, and you want to put the brakes on, but then again, even talented guys like Greg Norman hit near the pin and yank it back all the way off the green. Try and work on landing soft and rolling to the hole, rather than trying to spin back to it. If you have to spin the ball, do so by "clipping" it with the wrists locked, not by snapping your wrists.

TAKE IT BACK AS FAR AS YOU CAN. I can usually tell if a player's dropped off his game a bit by how far he takes the club back. One of the great misconceptions of golf instruction is that shortening the backswing is a cure for a lot of swing problems. I think it brings on more problems and especially causes people to get too fast. Keep your long backswing, or at least take it back to where it's parallel to the ground. Mother nature will shorten it up eventually anyway, but if you hurry up the process, you'll just hit the ball a lot less further and often times wind up with a swing that's too quick and jerky.

Also, don't be afraid of swinging hard. I don't mean consciously try to kill it. But I find that provided you don't jerk and get too quick at the takeaway or when you begin the downswing, you can get into the hitting area as hard as you want to. People look at pros and say, "his swing looks so smooth, so effortless," but when you slow the camera down, you can see some genuine clubhead speed going on there. Fred Couples may look like he's hardly swinging, but what you can't see is how he increases speed when the clubhead gets within a foot of the ball. Accelerate through that hitting area. One other swing thought—try and keep the same swing for every club. People differ on this, but the way I figured is, it's worked for Jack Nicklaus for over forty years and that's good enough for me.

DON'T BE A "DELIBERATE" PLAYER. Tour golf on TV has ruined it for all of us as far as pace of play. The pros, even if they shouldn't, may take a lot of time, but at least their livelihood depends on it. So does mine, yet I tend to play fast. But there are too many people out there everywhere who will put you to sleep with their drag-ass, methodical play, and there's just no reason for it. Many of them are hurting themselves and don't even know it. The way I see it, most people have a limited power of concentration. The longer you stand over a ball waiting to pull the trigger, the farther away you're gonna get from the original impulse, which is to hit the damn thing. Most people's concentration, mine included, is not so good that they can stand over a ball forever thinking about what they're supposed to do. No matter how fast you think you may be playing, go ahead and pick up the pace a little—you'll play that much better.

ADJUST FOR WIND. Playing so much Florida golf on windy courses, I learned the best way to hit through a gale just by watching great wind players like Tommy Bolt and Nate Starks. Wind players love a good, stiff breeze, since 90 percent of golfers fall to pieces mentally when the wind starts to kick up. The main thing I learned hitting upwind was to play the ball way back in your stance then drive through it with your hands to keep it down. By that I mean lead the left hand through lower, rather than let it come up. The lower you keep the hands, the lower the ball stays to the ground.

When you're playing downwind, play the ball forward in your stance, and tee it up a little higher than usual. This will help you make contact on the upswing and get you the height you need to get that sucker up and ridin' the jet stream.

ADJUST FOR DIFFERENT LIES. I've played a lot of golf on less-than-immaculate courses where you had to have a wide variety of shots. I've also seen many a player approach a tough lie with desperation—"Damn, I don't have this shot in my bag"—and that's death right there. Just the confidence of knowing how to strike any out-of-the-ordinary shot, no matter how difficult, is the first step towards getting it right.

Off of hardscrabble, hardpan, or any hard dirt, winter-type lie with no grass under or around the ball, I try to really slow down the swing and lead hard with my left hand to make sure that I catch the ball first and not the ground. Actually the best is to catch ball and dirt at the same time as close as possible to the point where the ball sits on the dirt. Keep the blade open on these shots and generally punch the irons. The hands shouldn't be the least bit flippy on this.

A lot of cussin' goes on when the rock winds up in a nasty ole' pea-patch divot. The best thing to do here is take one more club (say four-, instead of a five-iron), play the ball middle-stance with a little more weight on your left side and hit down on it. That will keep a lower trajectory and reduce the chance of chunking or mis-hitting the ball.

When your ball sits in deep rough, you want to make sure that you don't leave it in there. On a short shot, take a long swing and be sure you follow through; the ball will likely run, so if you don't have a lot of green to work with, let it go by the hole. On longer shots out of the rough, what I like to do is take two clubs less, swing hard, maybe even hood it just a bit (close the clubface) and force the ball out of there. Say I'm at normal seven-iron distance (for me); if the ball is in deep I'll muscle a nine-iron to cut through the grass so that the ball won't come out dead. From bad lies, the best mental approach is to forget about accuracy, and focus more on getting to a general area where you can stay alive and maybe halve the hole.

A long time ago, I took to playing golf for money, and even with my somewhat diminished skills today, it's still the only way I will play. I love this game, but if I'm not gonna play for a little something decent, I'd rather leave the sticks in the trunk. That's just the way it is with me.

If I have found one thing to be true over forty-some odd

years of gambling at golf, it's that natural ability alone won't make you a consistent winner. There's a lot of ways to skin a cat; I know, since I've been skinned enough myself to learn a few of those ways. But if you go through these wars long enough, you eventually learn how to take care of yourself so that you're the skinner instead of the skinee—most of the time. Let me share a few tips from the hustling side of golf that will hopefully help you stay on the plus side. The game is just one hell of a lot more fun that way.

HANDICAPPING. Golf bettors like to say that the majority of matches are won or lost on the first tee. In other words, the handicap or amount of strokes one player (or team) is getting will be too one-sided one way or another over eighteen holes for the other to overcome. The best way to keep from digging yourself a big hole before you even tee off, is to have a clear idea of how your opponent stacks up and at the same time try and stay honest with yourself in assessing your own game. Personally, I love to play where I feel that I know my opponent's game better than he himself does.

Too often, I think people subconsciously plan out their games based on the worst an opponent will possibly shoot against the best they themselves will score. That kind of figuring is a flat-out loser. If you've played with a guy a few times, you should be able to predict what he's likely to shoot. Factor that in with how you really play and that should tell you how many shots a side you should be getting (or giving).

I've found that the majority of golfers have "Hollywood" handicaps that make them out to be better players than they are—handicaps that don't accurately reflect their game. It's an ego thing, but most people misrepresent themselves by thinking they play better than they actually do, and it costs them when they come up against sandbaggers who will gladly take advantage. The handicap system is based on little more than scout's honor; it can get way out of whack when good players don't turn in their best scores and bad players leave out their skunkers.

Golfers insist on matching up based on what's on their "official" USGA handicap cards, but often, it'd be a whole lot fairer game if they negotiated a bet beforehand, based as closely as possible on their true skills. Then they could adjust from match to match, or even after nine holes, to keep things in line. Remember, a handicap card full of bogus scores is nothing but a license to steal. By the way, I've never had a handicap card.

MATCH PLAY—COURSE MANAGEMENT. Pro players put a great emphasis in knowing and practicing the course they're playing, and they should, since every stroke counts in medal play. But when you're going head-to-head in match play there's a different type of course management to look for, and that is how do various situations and holes affect you and/or your opponent? I generally always played full-blast, but I'm not crazy. If a certain hole gives me trouble consistently, I'll back off a little and just try and get my par. If that same hole gives my opponent trouble, I'll definitely back off. You should always note your opponent's weaknesses and take advantage accordingly, play them off your own strengths. This will help you decide how risky you want to play each hole and each shot. By the same token, if he seems to birdie any one hole more often than not, you certainly don't want to hold anything back.

I put a big premium on the money holes—the last three on every nine. I try to concentrate and stay relaxed even more on these holes, because I know that'll be the difference in a close match. If you've never played a course, and the game you've got means something, take a cart out ahead of time and go check out the 16th, 17th, and 18th holes—the landing area for drives, the approach angles, the pin placements, everything. That way, when you reach these holes, you'll be mentally prepared. Everybody's always got problems to work out—that's the name of the game. Relax, stay steady, and let the other guy stub his toe. In match play, how any two players handle the finishing holes usually decides who drowns and who doesn't.

GIMMES. I've got a game I play in sometimes in Charlotte where these tight-asses just will not give me a putt. I've had eight-inchers left, waited to hear somebody mumble, "that's good," only to have it get so quiet you could hear a rat pissing on cotton. I might have missed one of those a few years back, and they're still waiting for it to happen again. But it's a good mental practice to expect to have to putt everything out. Anyway, I will usually give anything around a foot in length, but not too much more than that.

If you're going to give putts, give 'em early and never late in a round. An old hustle, that I believe dates back to Walter Hagen, is to let an opponent pick up any number of two-, three-footers throughout the round, and then when a crucial tide-turnin', short money putt comes up, make him finish up. If a man has to can his first short putt in order to keep from dropping all the cheese late in a round, there's a good chance he might just freeze up like a Popsicle.

BETTING. People shouldn't really play for more than they can afford to lose, but most Sunday games aren't even close to getting to that point anyway. I always felt golfers should test themselves a little more than they usually do out on the course. You'll find nitty players with low-handicaps who won't bet more than $25 on their own skill on a round of golf; then they'll go bet a few hundred on a couple of football games and buy lottery tickets all week. It doesn't make sense to me.

Some of the individuals I've known with the most gamble are high handicappers—they may not play the greatest golf, but make them the right game at the right price and they'll jump in head first. For golfers who like to bet a bit, I would suggest that they take it right near the top of their limit, enough to keep the juices going, yet not too much to get the apple stuck in the throat. And if an on opponent appears to be too tough at a small game ($5–$10 nassaus), it's not a bad idea to try and kick up the stakes a bit and see if he might not start to quiver. Beware of the player with a nice swing who somehow loses a few early bets and wants to double the stakes at the turn. Don't be throwing that dog a bone.

On the subject of "pressing" (doubling up bets): press bets, where an additional, separate wager comes in at some point in the round (usually when one player is two holes down), are generally to the better golfer's advantage. As I mentioned earlier, the better player elevates his game a notch or two in the homestretch, and it's to his advantage to have as many bets going as possible. Naturally, if you're getting strokes on any part of the remaining holes, you'll want to press. And if your game is on fire, a fool may want to press you repeatedly to try and cool you off. Accommodate him and make him pay for it.

Now if a good player happens to be down three holes on the original bet and one on the press with only one hole remaining, he may ask for one more "closeout" press. In such cases, you'd have to be in a very generous mood to give it to him. By winning that last bet on one hole, he can wipe out his entire deficit; in reality, you're laying him 2–1 odds on the money on the final bet. You won't be the greatest sport in the world for turning down a closeout press, but it's smart golf. Don't be a lollipop.

CHEATING. People who cheat are usually running scared, which often times puts it in your favor depending on how much they're helping themselves. Now, if a guy's moving his ball around to good lies in the rough, that's tough to overcome. Propping the ball up for a sweet hit can make a stroke or two difference, depending on how bad it was sitting down. But it's a bad scene just on having to watch somebody, and it's embarrassing to have to deal with it if you're going to call it. By the same token, if I'm beating on a guy who's cheating me, there's no way I'm ever going to say anything to him or anybody else. It'll have to be our little secret.

However, if a guy's getting over on you by stealing an inch or so marking the ball on the green, I say let him do it for awhile—it probably won't make much difference anyway. Then, on an important putt late in the round, tell him to get back where he's supposed to be, and I guarantee you it will wreak some havoc on his head.

I recently played in a game with a guy who had an arrow painted on his ball, which he used to line up the direction of his putts. I knew it was illegal, but I didn't say boo about it. I really kind of like the idea of playing a man who putts so bad he's got to paint an arrow on his damn ball.

PARTNERS. The best thing you can do when you team up with somebody, whether it's for a tournament or a money match, is to make sure you're compatible, golfwise. Sometimes, based on strategy, you'll have to play a safe shot when you maybe don't want to—but you do it for the good of the team. When Dickie Starnes and I first hooked up, I was such a long hitter that I know it forced Dickie to be sure and lay it out safely in the fairway—the better to allow me to go ahead and crush it to increase our chances for bird. He never objected even if I did cause him to be a short hitter for awhile. Trust is real big here and I'm not talking about worrying about the money split or getting dumped on. I'm talking about respecting each other's abilities and not apologizing after every shot.

You never want to browbeat a partner (I love it when I see opposing teams breaking down this way). We all make mistakes in a round and how you come out of any match often depends on your ability to recover. Support is real important here, especially seeing as how in "best ball," it only takes but one player to carry the team on every hole. Everything you say should always be positive; if you notice something wrong in your partner's game, wait a couple of holes before you ever suggest anything. Unsolicited advice can destroy any good golf relationship.

CLUB SELECTION. One of the oldest tricks in the book is when a good player throws off his opponent by club selection. Typically, a player will grab, maybe, a four-iron on say a 160-yard par 3, make sure everybody knows it, then put some mystery swing on it and the ball ends up ten feet from the hole. Next thing you know, the others in the group are mis-clubbing and overshooting the green. Tommy Bolt was a master at this. He had a thousand-and-one shots with every stick in his bag, and he always made sure you saw exactly what he was hitting, knowing it would only screw you up.

The best thing I can tell you is don't be a bag-hawk. Everybody's got their own swing anyway, and I just don't think club information is half as important as people think it is. Different strokes for different folks is the way I look at it. One man's four-iron is another man's driver. Most of the time, if you go back to your bag to change after you peeped on what club somebody else selected, I'd say you're dead in the water. Just trust your own judgment.

PSYCH JOBS. Gamesmanship goes way back in golf, and it can get to be a real pain in the ass. People who run their mouths too much are usually underdogs looking for an edge. And people who are overly sensitive to any comments are setting themselves up to fail. I used to play with a guy who could not stand to hear the word "shank"—the power of suggestion was too much for him. Every time out, somebody, not me, would casually say, "Gee, I hope I don't shank this shot," and he would fall apart. "Why'd you have to bring that up?" he would moan, and spend the rest of the day shanking the ball.

I've had all kinds of garbage thrown my way. Crazy Cole used to jingle change when I was putting—he must have carried three, four dollars worth of coin in his pockets. I've had guys pull away in their golf cart on my downswing—"Oh I'm sorry, didn't mean to do that," they'd say. Others would come up with junk like, "Let me see that driver; has it always been so hook-faced?" Or they'd look at my putter and say, "this thing is so upright I don't know how you can putt with it." Anything to play on my mind.

With so much time put in on this game, I've trained myself to block out a great deal. But as much as I hate to admit it, some of it will still get to me. The talk—"are you swingin' faster than usual, Leon?," something like that—I've learned to shrug off. But when a guy's moving on the tee or when I putt, it can get to be distracting. Even if you say something, it's never going to completely stop. And that's the worst part—waiting for the distraction, just thinking about it is a distraction in itself. Sometimes, it may be an accident, but more often you're dealing with repeat offenders.

Ignoring it is easier said than done. Some people can even turn it back around. Somebody once said something to Sam Snead on the tee that he didn't like. "Don't mess with me, son," he said. "I've got a needle longer than your arm." But it can turn into a losing battle. Better to simply train yourself to block it out. And if that fails, you might want to look for another game—unless you have a loser on the hook, in which case you've just got to put up with the bullshit.

HUSTLERS. I know that in most parts of the worldwide golfing community, a hustler is thought of as a scratch player who hides behind a dirty little five- or six-handicap. You get plenty of those, but in my neck of the woods, a true golf hustler is a good player who can elevate his game against another good player when the money's up. Maybe he doesn't always show his very best game, but then again, he doesn't usually have to.

There are con-artists who will flat-out disguise their game. I've seen guys who couldn't swing a lick on the practice tee turn into Jack Nicklaus once the money was up. That never really bothered me 'cause I always figured to have the best of it anyway—long as we're playing even up. But there are things to look for, little clues to let you know who or what you're up against. For starters, if there's a one-iron in your opponent's bag with a spot the size of a quarter worn into the center of the grooves, you'd better bring your A-game. Tougher to check, but calluses on the underside of the left-hand grip fingers are a pretty good giveaway of a full-time player. Same thing if the glove hand is bleach white from never seeing the sun in twenty years.

At any level, what you have to watch out for are players who seem to bring it on just a few strokes better as the stakes increase, and also those players who quietly suggest a higher bet. I always considered myself in that company, but I've run into my share of tough customers, too. For the good golfer who's planning on giving up strokes to a stranger based on handicap, he should be careful when the opponent says he'll take fewer strokes for more money. I've been there before, and I usually wound up with way too much wood to chop.

MATCH PLAY. Every weekend, millions of golfers go out and play nassaus, skins or any number of hole-by-hole, man-to-man match play betting games. Too many times they hurt themselves by worrying about their overall scores and over-estimating their abilities (trying impossible shots) and not really paying attention to their match or what their opponents are doing. Recently, I've been going up against a player who's always wanting to break 70—seems like that's all he ever cares about. In a close finish, he puts that much more pressure on himself, which really makes it easier for me. Hell,

I've shot all the 61s in my life I could ever use; all I want to do at this point is take down the money.

When you really know the man you're golfing with, you should be aware of his body language. If he's getting impatient or a bit twitchy or quick with his swing, you should use that to steady your own game and let him self-destruct. Now if that same player is in a trance, a super relaxed zone where nothing seems to bother him, you might have to switch to overdrive just to catch him. Read your opponent, not just his scorecard.

In match play, you have to play to your strengths. If you're a long knocker playing a weaker hitter, use your power to advantage. Of course, if your opponent hits a ball out-of-bounds, play safe any way you can. But on the long par 4s, let 'er rip and put him at the disadvantage playing a long approach shot to your short one. Same thing with the par 5s—don't hold back. By the same token, if you're a short-but-straight hitter, exploit that part of your game. Don't try to hit with the big dog, which, in over-swinging, might rob you of your edge in accuracy. Let Fido swing for the fences and play from other fairways while you frustrate him with dead-center hits.

As I've stressed before, I like to focus on the last few holes, which I consider to be the money holes. But the most important thing that you can do in match play is to jump out in front as soon as possible. That puts you in control of the match and forces the other guy to play catch-up. That's when you may want to play more conservatively and match your opponent shot-for-shot. But here too, you want to be careful and not give him an opening. Some people can't stand to be behind; others get motivated by it. It's all a fine line, which means you have to be attentive to the other player and the situation.

When driving length is roughly the same, a rule of thumb in match play is that with equally-skilled players, the one who's furthest away and gets to hit first to the green has the advantage. Sam Snead used to make sure he was away, so he could flag it and put all the pressure on his opponent. Tiger Woods won his first tournament this way playing sudden death against Davis Love. Woods, who was longer off the tee, took less club and left himself slightly behind Love. He then snuck an eight-iron about twelve feet from the hole. Love followed up by yanking his approach into the trap.

Woods also used an old match-play tactic to his advantage when he "finished up" (instead of marking and waiting) after he ran his first putt a couple of feet by the hole. That meant he was in with his par, putting all that much more pressure on Love to sink his own nine-footer or lose. Too many people mark their ball after a lag putt. If you go ahead and knock it in, it can't help but squeeze the other guy a little. Also, you won't have to stand around thinking about missing it. If you get in the hole first, you may not necessarily win it, but at least you won't lose it.

I've saved the most important lesson for last. As much of a competitor as I am, as much as I want, even need to win playing golf, I do not consider myself a cutthroat player. I pride myself on the fact that I've been invited back to all (well, almost all) the games I've played in over the years, and I think that's generally because people enjoy playing with me—win or lose.

With a few exceptions, I have never tried to bury anybody or grab every last penny. Without exception, I've never tried to hurt anybody's feelings. I tend to console people when they lose and try not to piss and moan too much when I lose. It may sound self-serving—and actually it is—but I enjoy being nice.

Even to a golf hustler, the most gratifying side-benefits of the game are meeting people and making friends. Since this is the most social sport there is, I think everyone—from hackers to pros—should work on making the most of that. Golf works out best when everybody treats it like the gentleman's game it's supposed to be—especially when you're gambling. The 19th hole is no place for sore losers and sour winners. It's never too late to start having fun. So don't let that ego get in the way of enjoying the greatest game there is, and remember, you can't always win.

A Guide to Golf's Gambling Games

You don't have to be Leon Crump (or Michael Jordan, for that matter) to enjoy a friendly wager out on the golf course. One of the most ingenious aspects to golfing competition is the variety of methods that have been devised over the years to gamble at the game. In this spirit, millions of golfers who may never break par, try to trim each other for a few bucks on any given weekend. The following is an assortment of different games at which golfers can regularly play and bet on:

AIR PRESS

By calling out "air press" at any time, Player A may challenge Player B to an additional bet on a hole while Player B's shot is in the air. Player B must accept the bet before the ball stops rolling or lose one half the designated amount. Player B may of course return the favor when it is Player A's turn to hit.

ALTERNATE SHOT (SCOTCH FOURSOMES)

Two teams tee off with golfers playing alternate shots on one ball per team. In some cases rules allow for all four players to tee off, and each team then selects which ball to play alternately, with the second shots to be played by the golfers whose drives were rejected.

BEST BALL

A game by which any one player tries to beat the "best" ball (or score) of the other two or three golfers in his group. "Best ball" is also commonly known as the way two teams may play each other, with the lowest number of shots on any hole by a golfer representing that team's recorded score.

BINGO, BANGO, BONGO

There are three separate ways to score on each hole:

BINGO: first on the green.

BANGO: nearest to the pin.

BONGO: first in the cup.

It's very important to fairness that the golfer who's away always hits or putts first. While this game isn't usually played by serious golf bettors, it works well for foursomes comprised of low-rollers with diverse handicaps.

BISQUES

Handicap strokes are generally allotted on a course's toughest holes. But in Bisques, rather than receive strokes on preset holes, a player may use those strokes ("bisques") at any point he wishes, provided he announces it before the particular hole. This game is for those golfers who, after regularly losing to birdies on tough par 5, might using their extra shots on the easier par-3 holes.

BLITZ

A foursome splits into two teams, with each team playing for a maximum of six possible points (dollars?) per hole. One point awarded for closest to the pin, one for birdie, one for fewest putts, one for lower total of combined scores and two points for low ball in the group. Earning all six points on a hole is called a "blitz," which results in doubling the winning amount.

BRIDGE

Playing on two-man teams, golfers bid on every tee, according to their projected total strokes for the upcoming hole. Any bid is followed either by a "pass," a lower bid, or a "double," if one team feels strongly that the other team can't shoot what was bid. A word of advice: Drop this game if you're slowing down the people behind you.

CALCUTTA

A pool of moneys collected by auctioning off teams of players in a tournament. The total is ultimately split into percentages, rewarding those who backed the top finishers. Before the tournament starts, players generally have the option to purchase for themselves up to half of the amount bid on their team. Calcuttas used to be common at PGA Tour stops, before the USGA voiced strong disapproval.

CATS AND DOGS

The single lowest score (the "cat") collects on each hole, while the single highest score (the "dog") has to pay up, in this game played within foursomes. Ties are carried over to the following hole. The only problem with this format is in theoretically leaving two golfers out of the action on every hole.

CROSS-COUNTRY

The idea here is to play total strokes for a predetermined distance across a golf course, all the way from one tee to another hole, usually at opposite ends of the course. Cross-country is often played in foul weather or in near-darkness, to avoid interfering with regular play.

GARBAGE

Often bet along with "Skins" games, Garbage rewards the following:

GREENIES: on the green, closest to the pin on par-3s.

SANDIES: saving par with one putt after being in a sand trap.

CHIPPIES: chipping in the hole from anywhere off the green.

SHARKIES: saving par after being in a water hazard.

HORSE RACE (SHOOT-OUT)

Play begins with any number of golfers, all in the same group, from the same tee. As each hole is played, the player (or players) with the highest score is eliminated. The object is to wind up as the last "horse" running. Chipping contests may be used as tie-breakers on each hole.

LOW-BALL

A four-man teams game, played for two points on each hole, one for the lowest score and one for the lowest team total. No points given for ties.

LOW-HIGH (HIGH-LOW)

Another teams game, two points on every hole—one for lowest score and, in this case, one for the lower of the two high scores. Example: if a team with Players A and B shoots a three and a five against two fours for Players C and D, then each team would get one point on that hole—the score of three being the outright winner for one point, and the four beating five for the other. This game is a good equalizer to keep the team with the best player from automatically winning.

MATCH PLAY

The general overall category of hole-by-hole competition between individuals or teams. Tied holes are called "halves"; a match is termed "dormie" when one player is leading by as many holes as remain to be played; and a match is considered "closed out" when a player or team has won more holes than remain to be played. Strict eighteen-hole match play is the oldest competition in golf.

MULLIGAN

An allowance for another tee shot (with no penalty), usually after a muffed effort. By some stipulations, one mulligan is permitted per nine holes, by others, only on the first tee. The USGA Rules of the Game make no such allowances.

NASSAU

The most common and popular of all links action, a nassau is comprised of three separate bets for eighteen holes. Using a match play format, players compete for most holes won on the front nine, the back nine, and the overall round. Sometimes nassaus are played "four-ways" or "five-ways," meaning that the front nine is worth one unit, and the back nine and/or overall are worth two units.

PRESS BETS

The "press" is a separate bet made by a losing player (or side) at any point during a round. Presses cover the remaining holes to be played on the nine, and are usually made when a player is two holes down. A press bet doesn't have to be accepted by the player ahead, although turning one down can be considered poor form. For avoiding bad blood, automatic, two-down presses are recommended.

RABBIT

The first player to win a hole holds the "rabbit" for the bet. To take away the rabbit (and the dollars), another player must win a subsequent hole outright, at which point the bet doubles. The money only goes to the player holding the rabbit after the 9th and 18th holes.

ROUND-ROBIN

For golfers with varied handicaps, this game insures fairness by having partners change teams every six holes. Using match play format, three separate matches are played among four players for holes 1–6, 7–12, and 13–18.

SCRAMBLE (CAPTAIN'S CHOICE)

A common game, generally played with four-man teams, against any number of other four-man teams. On every hole, all players tee off, the best drive is selected and each golfer hits from that spot. The procedure is repeated (going to the best shot, with everybody hitting) until the ball is in the hole. Most scramble formats include a stipulation that every player must contribute a minimum of two drives during any given round.

SEVEN-UP

A devious little game, played over a set number of holes on the putting green, at which any number of players may take part. Two points are awarded for a hole-in-one, one point for being closest to the hole, and two points are subtracted for three-putting. First to seven wins. Always takes longer than expected.

SKINS

Every hole has a dollar value, or a "skin," which is won by the lowest score. If two players tie, all tie, and the following hole becomes a "carry-over" of double value, and so on (triple, quadruple) until one golfer wins. The two-tie–all-tie aspect makes for brief camaraderie when one player ties the other low scorer, in effect "saving" the hole for the other two.

SNAKE

A side-bet on putting that penalizes any golfer who three-putts. The first golfer who does so holds the "snake" until another golfer three-putts, at which point the snake changes hands. The player holding the snake after nine and eighteen holes pays the others.

STABLEFORD

Using full handicap, players win points for net scores, which are totalled after eighteen holes. Point values may vary, but the standard version goes eagle=four points, birdie=three points, par=two points, and bogie=one point.

STRING

Each player is given a length of string corresponding to his handicap before a round. The higher the handicap, the longer the string. At any time during the round, he may use part or all of the string to get relief from a bad lie or credit for a missed putt. String is proportionally cut down and discarded during play.

STROKE PLAY (MEDAL)

Arguably the most conservative format, the scoring standard used in professional and most championship golf—total of fewest strokes at the end of eighteen holes wins.

VEGAS

Two-man teams combine scores per hole and pay off on the differential. Example: Team A shoots a four and a five on a hole where Team B shoots five and seven. Team A would score 45 on the hole, whereas Team B would have 57 and lose twelve units. Caution: This game can get very expensive.

WOLF

A fixed order is set on the first tee among four players and maintained the entire round. Player A leads off as "wolf," and based on the other players' drives, selects a partner for that hole only. Player B is wolf on the second hole, and so on, and units won are totalled at the end. At any time, a player who is wolf may choose to be "lone wolf" and play that hole against the other three for triple the stakes.

YARD GOLF

The unit of wager is decided according to the length of each hole. For example, at a dollar a yard, a 370-yard hole would be worth $370 to the winner.

Acknowledgments

Any book of this nature relies a great deal on the contributions of other players in helping recall and verify past events. For all their generous support and for their assistance in hashing over stories recent and old, the authors would like to thank the following people:

Dickie Starnes, Robert Anderson, Fred Barnes, Tommy Barr, Jack Binyon, James Black, Tommy Bolt, Bob Bryant, Marshall "Squirrel" Carpenter, Hubert Crump, John Gilbert, G.T. Godwin, J.C. Goosie, John Ham, Bill Harvey, Terry Heles, Jack Hemric, Mark Henderson, Johnny Lewis, Jimmy Mann, Charlie Miller, Phil O'Neal, Horace "Catfish" Phillips, Frank Reynolds, Scott Salzer, Sparky, Frank Stone, Eddie Thompson, Willie West, Phil Wheeler, and Larry Young.

Also, major thanks to the Eastwood Golf Course, to Alvin London, to our agent, Chris Calhoun, and to our editor, Eamon Dolan.